LEADING
Modern
Learning

A Blueprint for **Vision-Driven** *Schools*

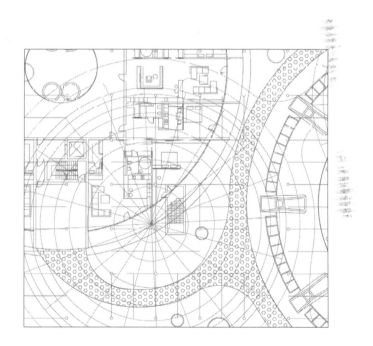

Jay McTighe | Greg Curtis
Foreword by Yong Zhao

Solution Tree | Press a division of
Solution Tree

555 North Morton Street
Bloomington, IN 47404
800.733.6786 (toll free) / 812.336.7700
FAX: 812.336.7790
email: info@solution-tree.com
solution-tree.com

Visit **go.solution-tree.com/leadership** to download the reproducibles in this book.

Printed in the United States of America

19 18 17 16 15   1 2 3 4 5

Library of Congress Cataloging-in-Publication Data

McTighe, Jay.

Leading modern learning : a blueprint for vision-driven schools / by Jay McTighe and Greg Curtis.

pages cm

Includes bibliographical references and index.

ISBN 978-1-936764-70-9 (perfect bound) 1. School improvement programs--United States. 2. Educational change--United States. 3. School management and organization--United States. I. Curtis, Greg, 1950- II. Title.

LB2822.82.M395 2016

371.2'07--dc23

2015018700

Solution Tree
Jeffrey C. Jones, CEO
Edmund M. Ackerman, President

Solution Tree Press
President: Douglas M. Rife
Senior Acquisitions Editor: Amy Rubenstein
Editorial Director: Lesley Bolton
Managing Production Editor: Caroline Weiss
Production Editor: Rachel Rosolina
Copy Editor: Sarah Payne-Mills
Proofreader: Jessi Finn
Text and Cover Designer: Rian Anderson
Compositor: Abigail Bowen

We dedicate this book to the memory
of Dr. Grant Wiggins (1950–2015).
Grant was an intellectual force and
beloved friend who challenged educators
to question the status quo, examine
"unthinking habits," envision the
future, and always plan with the end
in mind. While no longer with us,
his influence permeates the book.

What the Experts Are Saying About
Leading Modern Learning

"Making a remarkably timely contribution to the modernization of learning organizations, McTighe and Curtis provide clear and creative guidance on how to move from 'old school' to new. The transition is a challenging one, requiring specifics on operationalizing fresh visions coupled with practical, realistic steps. Administrators, teachers, curriculum designers, and community members will find solutions and imaginative possibilities here. *Learning Modern Learning: A Blueprint for Vision-Driven Schools* is a must-read for the right-now educator."

—Heidi Hayes Jacobs, Author, Director of Curriculum 21 Project

"A bridge to a more compelling educational future, this book is both aspirational and practical. It sketches out a modern view of teaching and learning, then creates a blueprint for building to the vision. It is a primer for forward-looking educators."

—Carol Ann Tomlinson, William Clay Parrish, Jr. Professor and Chair of Educational Leadership, Foundations, and Policy; Curry School of Education; University of Virginia

"School staffs and educational leaders wishing to modernize their curriculum will profit from following the logical and detailed processes offered in this practical guide to curriculum design. It is built around three essential curriculum decisions: what's worth learning (outcomes), how to determine if the outcomes have been achieved (assessment), and what instructional strategies best facilitate students acquiring those outcomes (instruction). It all starts, however, with creating and committing to a vision—not only for learners and schools but also for a more thought-full world."

—Art Costa, Professor Emeritus, California State University, Sacramento

"This book offers a practical and much needed set of strategies that accompanies a thoughtful framework for considering the change process. Regardless of the programs you may be considering, the process is spelled out from vision and mission straight through to curriculum, instruction, and assessment. Regardless of where you are in the process, the ideas serve as a way of centering the work. Thanks, Jay and Greg, for systemic thinking by design!"

—Bena Kallick, Cofounder and Codirector of Institute for Habits of Mind, Program Director for Eduplanet21.com

"The one certainty for which we must prepare students now and in the future is change. This book offers a powerful, systemic framework for guiding educators in the move from vision to action in school revitalization. Practical strategies, tools, and examples guide the evolution of a modern learning institution toward greater relevance, authenticity, and personalization to best prepare today's learners for the challenges and opportunities of the future."

—Judy Willis, Neurologist, Former Teacher, Neuroeducation Speaker

"An amazing tool for schools—clear, practical, and intentional. *Leading Modern Learning: A Blueprint for Vision-Driven Schools* will empower schools to move toward excellence through a deliberate process by providing a complete blueprint designed to impact student learning from every element of the school experience. From vision to mission, learning targets, authentic assessment, and instruction—a complete system."

—Gail Seay, Director of Teaching and Learning, American School of Doha, Qatar

"This book provides a fresh way of looking at how we define and prioritize the kind of schooling we want for our contemporary learners. The combination of theory, practical tools, and exemplars makes this an engaging and effective book for educational leaders around the globe."

—Elizabeth Rossini, Director of Curriculum and Professional Learning, International School Bangkok

"Education leaders understand that today's challenges require fundamental changes to teaching and learning. But what is the best path? Jay McTighe and Greg Curtis have provided a much-needed roadmap in *Leading Modern Learning*. This book is destined to become the North Star for those seeking transformed classrooms."

—Ken Kay, CEO, and Valerie Greenhill, CLO, EdLeader21

Acknowledgments

Thank you to our editors and support people at Solution Tree, namely Rachel Rosolina, Lesley Bolton, and Caroline Weiss. You were a pleasure to work with!

Greg Curtis would like to acknowledge his wife, Cindy, and his two sons, Max and Ethan, for putting up with him through this process, as well as Martin Klopper and David Grim of Leadership Development International for the work that led to the Input-Output-Impact® model during their collaboration.

Solution Tree Press would like to thank the following reviewers:

Cynthia Matte
Assistant Superintendent
SAU 41
Hollis, New Hampshire

Kelly Schofield
Principal
Dana Elementary School
Hendersonville, North Carolina

Bob Shirley
Head of School
Woodlawn School
Davidson, North Carolina

Don Smith
Principal
Fond du Lac STEM Academy and
    Fond du Lac STEM Institute
Fond du Lac District Coordinator of
    Assessment
Fond du Lac, Wisconsin

Dana Tabor
Associate Principal for Instruction
Carl Wunsche Senior High School
Spring, Texas

Visit **go.solution-tree.com/leadership** to download
the reproducibles in this book.

Table of Contents

About the Authors

Jay McTighe is an accomplished author, having coauthored thirteen books, including the award-winning and best-selling *Understanding by Design* series with Grant Wiggins. His books have been translated into fourteen languages. Jay has also written more than thirty-five articles and book chapters and has been published in leading journals, including *Educational Leadership* and *Education Week*. Jay has an extensive background in professional development and is a regular speaker at national, state, and district conferences and workshops. He has presented in forty-seven states within the United States, in seven Canadian provinces, and internationally in thirty-three countries on six continents. To learn more about Jay's work, visit www.jaymctighe.com or follow @jaymctighe on Twitter.

Greg Curtis is an author and independent educational consultant. He is currently based in Beijing and has spent much of his career working with schools around the world in systemwide capacities. Greg has been a technology director, a curriculum and professional learning director, and a strategic planner for international schools in Europe and Asia. He also works with organizations such as EdLeader21, the New England Association of Schools and Colleges, Jay McTighe & Associates Educational Consulting, EduTect Inc., and several schools and districts around the world. His work focuses on long-term, systems-based change and strategic improvement in schools and districts around impacts and modern learning. He is also a coauthor of *Learning Personalized: The Evolution of the Contemporary Classroom* with Allison Zmuda and Diane Ullman. To learn more about Greg's work, visit www.gregcurtis-consulting.ca or follow @jgcurtis on Twitter.

To book Jay McTighe or Greg Curtis for professional development, contact pd@solution-tree.com.

Foreword

By Yong Zhao

The 21st century was once the distant future. Hence *21st century* used to be a popular phrase for marketing products, ideas, and policies by evoking hopes and fears that may eventually exist. As a result, 21st century education has become a vision that compels bold actions—actions that ensure a safe departure from the past and guarantee success in the future.

The 21st century has arrived. The once-distant future has become our reality. While 21st century education has gained a diverse set of definitions that transcend the scientific meaning of *21st century* as simply a reference of time, conversations about 21st century education can no longer be futuristic, driven by bold claims, fanciful imaginations, or fearmongering rhetoric. It is no longer meaningful to argue why we need or why we do not need 21st century education, nor is it productive to continue the debate over how 21st century education may differ from the education in the 20th, 19th, or 15th century.

It is time that we delivered a modern education that both meets the challenges and takes advantage of the realities of the 21st century. This is, however, not an easy task, because while we are living in the 21st century, the institution of education started in the 19th or 20th century. It was built to meet the challenges of the past. It was built with the resources we had before. And once it was built, we spent the last century perfecting it. As Winston Churchill said, "we shape our buildings; thereafter they shape us"—our education mindset has been shaped by the already-built institution.

This mindset accompanied us into the 21st century. It continues as a persistent force that shapes our views and defines our actions in education. In essence, we are prisoners of the past. To create a modern institution of education, we have to escape from the past first. We have to look at education with a fresh perspective, a new mindset. This new mindset must be grounded in today's realities, yesterday's lessons, and tomorrow's possibilities. The new education must start with the most recent discoveries about human beings: why they learn, how they learn, and where they learn. It must take into consideration the resources we have today, all the learning opportunities that can be harnessed in a globally connected society. It must also consider new outcomes—people not only able to cope with the 21st century but also able to create a better future for all.

However, we cannot flip a switch and change our mindset instantly. It takes time to change. But just spending time waiting for the arrival of a new mindset also does not work. We need to engage in real actions that are neither random nor sporadic. They need to be well organized, carefully designed, and deliberately planned. They also need to be understood and undertaken by all members of an education community. For this to happen, we need a blueprint, just like the blueprints that architects create to guide the construction of modern buildings.

This is just what Jay McTighe and Greg Curtis offer in this text: a blueprint for modernizing education.

Jay and Greg present a design process schools can follow to redesign education for 21st century learning. The process guides schools to engage in strategic moves that can ultimately lead to a new type of education needed for the 21st century. From vision to mission and from mission to action, Jay and Greg lay out a systematic process of redesigning schools with abundant evidence, proven strategies, and practical tools.

To be sure, this is not the first book I have seen that claims to provide practical guidance to education redesign. I have seen plenty of "blueprints" in education, and not all are equal; they can be good or bad. What makes me think this is a good blueprint is much more than the extensive practical strategies and actions. It is the sound research base behind the suggested strategies and actions and the ambitious goals these strategies and actions can help achieve. But most important, it is the bridge Jay and Greg build between distant, abstract, and grand ambitions and present, immediate, and small steps. They make the daunting task of designing a brand-new education achievable. It gives me, and all who desire a better education, confidence.

A blueprint can run the danger of being overly prescriptive and imposing a uniform view. As we know too well, educational institutions differ a great deal, as do people's views of what constitutes 21st century education—outcomes, processes, institutional structures, students' experiences, and pedagogy. For example, while I agree with Jay and Greg, I do think education should push even further in the areas of student autonomy and personalization as well as turning schools into global campuses. Still, Jay and Greg deal with these issues masterfully. While they have their version of a curriculum blueprint, assessment framework, and pedagogical approach for the 21st century, they do not impose them. I treat them as examples rather than as prescriptions. The process they suggest is about helping each individual school develop its own vision and mission. It is about schools working out strategies and actions of their own.

Education is in the futures business in that it is responsible for preparing students to live successfully in the future, however success is defined. But it should not be about preparing them to cope with the future or simply wait for the arrival of the future. It should be preparing them to proactively create the future. To train future-creators, we need future-oriented educational institutions, which are drastically different from institutions of the past and present. To create future-oriented educational institutions, we need to have a process, a plan, and a set of tools. This book offers such a blueprint, and an excellent one at that.

Introduction

Many researchers and authors, both within the field of education and beyond, have made the case for educational change to prepare today's students for the challenges and opportunities they will encounter tomorrow. Indeed, the press for 21st century schools has flourished for years under various names. We will not rehash the arguments, nor try to make the case. Rather, we begin with the simple premise that education needs to undertake major reform to meet the needs of our students, our countries, and our planet in the years to come. If you do not agree with this basic premise, we doubt this book is for you. However, if you agree that the world is changing and that educational institutions are obligated to acknowledge and address the future, read on.

In fact, the term *21st century learning* has itself become something of a cliché. And, as with many clichés, it can sometimes be dismissed as "been there, done that," thereby losing some of its original potential as an agent of change. We use the term *modern learning* interchangeably with *21st century learning* to highlight the fact that we are not simply writing about implementing a trend but outlining ways in which education can remain relevant and learning can remain vital and connected with the future.

This book examines a central question: How might we determine and enact needed educational changes in a systemic and lasting way? Our contribution focuses on process. We offer a blueprint of practical and proven approaches to redesign your educational environment, whether a district, school, or single department. The methods we suggest have all been used in a variety of contexts. While you may have heard of them and even used some, it is our contention that these approaches are unlikely to lead to substantial change on their own. While each can add value, their transformative power will be realized collectively.

About This Book

We have organized this book into seven chapters framed by guiding questions. The first three chapters take us from vision to mission to action and introduce two frameworks—Input-Output-Impact® (IOI) and backward design—that we employ throughout the book. The next four chapters look at four critical components of any comprehensive educational system, namely curriculum, assessment, instruction, and reporting.

There is a logic to the arrangement of these chapters, and you should consider the book as describing a series of linked steps. While you may want to concentrate on certain chapters that most directly align with your interests, the premise outlined in the first few chapters is central to the alignment of all the components discussed in subsequent chapters. In fact, one of the goals of this book is to encourage a systemic approach to school change and improvement.

We recommend that district and school teams read this book together so that the work of different team members can be better linked and mutually supporting. Each chapter is framed by a guiding question to focus readers' attention and stimulate thinking and discussion.

Following is a brief overview of each chapter.

Chapter 1: The Power of Visioning

How do we develop a bold and compelling vision for modern learning?

While we cannot predict the future, we can examine the various trends and drivers of change that lead to an informed vision of a preferred future. We describe tangible strategies and practical protocols for engaging school communities in establishing a clear and compelling vision for modern learning.

Chapter 2: From Vision to Mission

How do we concretize our vision for modern learning into an actionable mission?

An educational mission declares an educational institution's values and specifies what it purports to achieve in terms of students' accomplishments. We describe the qualities of a futures-oriented educational mission and introduce the Input-Output-Impact framework (Curtis, 2015) to help us distinguish means from ends and always keep the end in mind.

Chapter 3: From Mission to Action

How do we collaboratively plan backward from desired results to purposeful actions?

Many powerful visions and missions are undone by the inability to translate great intentions into purposeful actions. The ideas of *Schooling by Design* (Wiggins & McTighe, 2007) provide a systemic framework for planning backward from a vision of a preferred future for your institution to a series of actions to realize it. In this chapter, we present a three-stage backward design process with a corresponding template to guide your strategic actions.

Chapter 4: Curriculum for Modern Learning

What are the building blocks for 21st century curricula, and how do we develop them?

A key element in achieving your mission is the development of a curriculum blueprint. The curriculum we propose emphasizes the development of conceptual understandings and the capabilities to transfer learning, which are key outcomes of 21st century schooling.

Chapter 5: An Assessment System for Modern Learning

How do we assess both disciplinary and transdisciplinary achievements?

Too often, 21st century skills fall through the cracks of conventional testing of academic content. Indeed, one of the most frequently missing elements of a school's reform effort is a rich and comprehensive assessment system that captures evidence of modern learning, not simply content acquisition. We show a process for grafting 21st century outcomes onto performance assessments to ensure that *everything* we proclaim to value is appropriately assessed.

Chapter 6: Instruction for Modern Learning

How do we align instruction practices, resources, and tools with our goals for modern learning?

Teaching is a means to an end. Clarity influences the nature and practice of the learning experiences needed to reach the end goals from your mission. In chapter 6, we explore the value of an established set of learning principles to guide the selection of teaching strategies and learning resources, and we describe the Acquisition, Meaning Making, Transfer (AMT) framework.

Chapter 7: A Reporting System for Modern Learning

How do we communicate student achievement and growth of modern learning?

Traditional grading practices and report cards are inadequate for reporting on 21st century learning. We explore an alternative grading system and a digital LearningBoard platform that better communicate student growth and achievement of our mission for modern learning.

In addition, in the appendices (page 147), we have included lists of recommended resources organized around key categories.

In this book, we seek to support meaningful reform through practical methods, and we are confident that the strategies and tools outlined here are replicable and scalable in varied school settings and contexts. We believe that these steps can be applied in multiple contexts, both large and small. Individually, they are achievable implementation steps for your 21st century vision. Collectively, they will make your vision come to life.

CHAPTER 1
The Power of Visioning

How do we develop a bold and compelling vision for modern learning?

A clear, compelling, and shared vision of what a district or school would like to achieve for its students in the future should anchor any plan for revitalizing schools. However, the word *vision* has widely differing interpretations. Educators use it to characterize everything from a simple, isolated idea to an almost mystical inspiration for a whole new reality. Our conception of a vision lies somewhere in between. We are not talking about vision as merely a statement but rather as a guiding process. *Visioning* is an essential first step in sharpening the focus and garnering the commitment needed for broad and meaningful change.

But aren't all visions directed toward the future? In a word, no. As noted in the introduction, we believe that an impediment to deep and lasting reform of education systems stems from our inability to envision a compelling future of a truly modern learning environment. Too often, school visions and the strategies developed to meet them are really concerned with fixing the present as opposed to creating the future. If our aspirations do not spring from the understandings gained through an informed inquiry into the future, our students are likely to be constrained to an education rooted in the past.

A truly futures-oriented vision gets us to the future more directly. If real change is going to happen within our schools, we believe that we need to leapfrog the present and get right to the future. Consider how China leapfrogged from a primitive telecommunications infrastructure straight to mobile phones. If it had plodded along the traditional path of constructing traditional telephone landlines, this transformation would have taken decades. It is time for schools to consider meaningful leaps rather than tentatively tiptoeing forward.

Overcoming a Fear of the Future

A willingness to embrace the future requires courage. Former U.S. President Ronald Reagan observed that "the future doesn't belong to the fainthearted; it belongs to the brave" (as cited in Milton, 2005, p. 85). Indeed, many people fear the unknown, and the future is essentially unknowable. A fear of the future can trigger predictable impulses: a desire to return to the comfort of the past, the inclination to remain frozen in the present, or the spark to fight any and all change. Indeed, the human brain is wired with this fight-flight-or-freeze response to fear and stress. Yet, we should bravely face the future, since returning to the past or stubbornly fighting to preserve the status quo will not result in the kind of contemporary education our students deserve.

It is important to stress that futures-oriented visioning is *not* about predicting the future. Predicting the future is, and always has been, a losing proposition. Yet, while there is no single future we can identify with any certainty, there are a number of potential futures that may emerge over time. Our quest is to recognize the various drivers of change that will impact education and learning. From there, we can develop a better understanding of the potential effects these catalysts may have on the process of schooling and choose a desired future to pursue.

Creating a Futures-Oriented Vision

Futures-oriented visioning can take many forms. We prefer a relatively simple, three-part process to help articulate the seeds of a compelling and accessible vision, as depicted in figure 1.1.

Figure 1.1: A futures-oriented visioning process.

Developing a Knowledge Base and a Future Orientation

A knowledge base is the necessary starting point for effective futures-oriented visioning. It allows an education community to engage in a positive and knowledgeable dialogue about the future and the concomitant education preparation. We cannot rest on existing perceptions, simple generalizations, preconceptions, or our own past experiences with education. A solid knowledge base about the trends and drivers of change in the future helps the community gain the understanding necessary to develop foresight about the many potential and emerging futures and the articulation of a desired future.

Here, we are in luck. Much has been researched and written about the future and, in particular, about the future of teaching and learning. Popular books abound on the subject, both in mainstream publishing and within the field of education. There are also organizations doing futures-oriented research, and their work adds great value to our understanding of the ways in which the future may evolve and emerge; they look beyond the knowable future (the next few years) and provide the foresight needed for the rest of us to engage in long-term developments. One such organization is KnowledgeWorks, which is best known for developing seminal documents such as the *2006–2016 Map of Future Forces Affecting Education* (KnowledgeWorks Foundation, 2006), *2020 Forecast: Creating the Future of Learning* (KnowledgeWorks Foundation, 2008), and *KnowledgeWorks Forecast 3.0: Recombinant Education—Regenerating the Learning Ecosystem* (KnowledgeWorks, 2012). Since its inception in 2000, KnowledgeWorks has contributed notable research and thought leadership around the trends and drivers of change affecting education. See appendix A for similar organizations.

The development of a knowledge base and a futures orientation offers a rich opportunity to engage different elements of your community in a futures-focused dialogue. Involvement of various school constituents is key, and a plan to engage members of your community appropriately and inclusively is an important part of the futures-oriented visioning process. For example, you might enlist a speaker for a professional development day or an evening meeting for parents. Or you could initiate a study group or book club with teachers. Viewing a series of thought-provoking, futures-oriented TED Talks would also be a stimulating way to enlist staff and parents in the process. Additionally, be sure to engage students, as they are generally keen to talk about their future. Through deep, rich, and collaborative engagement, we can inform the hearts *and* minds of our communities with an eye to the future.

However, consider this cautionary note: it is important to develop a knowledge base *before* continuing to the next step and actually generating a vision. Without a knowledge base, we cannot develop our preferred future with understanding or intent. In the absence of solid information, input is likely to be all over the map and impossible to forge into a unifying vision, and you are likely to end up with a wide variety of personal perceptions (some informed, some not), assertions based on false assumptions and misunderstandings, and contradicting points of view that are *not* drawn from evidence or research. Assumption and personal preference without real knowledge or understanding will not provide a foundation for developing the shared vision we seek.

Generating a Vision of the Preferred Future

As early as the 1950s, the U.S. military developed scenarios to discuss possible future situations. However, the business world didn't use the term *scenario-based planning* until the early 1970s when Royal Dutch Shell applied the process to address the energy crisis and the drastic changes confronting the oil and gas industry (Wack, 1985). At the time, scenario-based planning was a bold departure from the strategic planning processes that businesses typically used, and it worked. This process helps businesses explore possible emerging futures in various arenas for the sake of risk mitigation. Companies and organizations use the process to develop the insights necessary to react to the realities of emerging futures.

For our purposes, the term *scenario building* characterizes a process for examining the interplay of various trends and drivers of change and the countless potential futures that may emerge. Like a kaleidoscope twisting and turning bits of colored glass to form new combinations, different scenarios are held up to the light and turned this way and that to help us imagine a variety of possibilities.

Once you have engaged constituents in knowledge base–building activities (research, book clubs, dialogue, and cross-participant presentations) and have defined any necessary areas of inquiry (technology, funding, and globalization), we recommend the following scenario-building process.

- Identify (or provide) a set of polarities to examine.
- Graph the potential futures.
- Discuss the potential futures to decide on the preferred futures.

After we discuss the scenario-building process, we will detail how to facilitate it across a group of any size. Participation depends on the context. Smaller groups (such as a department or grade-level team) should involve all members, while a larger school or district should involve a representative group from across the community.

Identifying Polarities

By inquiring into trends and drivers of change, we can develop polarities that represent a span of possible characteristics of the future environment. For example, some of the pressures and realities of 21st century education could push education to become more *standardized* on one hand or highly *personalized* on the other. Other influences, like technology in conjunction with standardization, could cause learning to be derived from a *single source* (such as teachers in a brick-and-mortar school building) or from *multiple sources* (such as online tutorials, mentors, internships, and independent projects). See figure 1.2 (page 10) for a visual representation of these polarities with their representative questions.

Standardized

Personalized

Will learning be delivered through efficient mass modes or experienced in more personalized ways?

Single Sourced

Multisourced

Will schools dictate the primary sources of learning, or will students access learning resources from many suppliers?

Figure 1.2: Two polarities.

Simple polarities help us explore the numerous ways in which the future of education could unfold. Identifying these polarities is an important part of moving from developing a knowledge base to designing a preferred future. Table 1.1 presents potential polarities and accompanying questions.

To see how these polarities and their accompanying questions relate to one another and to the potential futures, we use a simple graphing technique.

Graphing the Potential Futures

When two sets of polarities are plotted on a four-quadrant chart (sometimes called a *magic square* but more properly known as a *Cartesian plane*) with accompanying questions, we can explore the various potential scenarios. We have found that the charts serve to stimulate thinking and prompt rich conversations about the possible futures suggested within each quadrant. Using the polarities discussed in figure 1.2—*standardized* versus *personalized* and *single sourced* versus *multisourced*—we've created the chart in figure 1.3 (page 12).

Table 1.1: Polarities and Sample Questions

Polarities	Sample Questions
Local versus global	Will learning focus on local or national contexts or adopt a global perspective?
Public sector versus corporate sector	Is the public school model going to remain the same, or is the private sector going to become more involved?
Career readiness versus college readiness	Should students be prepared for work or for institutions of higher education?
Career oriented versus citizenship oriented	Is learning geared toward college and career orientation or toward citizenship and satisfying, productive lives?
Specialized versus generalized	Should students gain deep knowledge in a few specialized areas or learn across a broader spectrum?
Short-term accountability versus long-term goals	Do we focus on short-term accountability measures or on long-term goals that may be more difficult to assess?
Disciplinary knowledge versus transdisciplinary skills	Do we educate for acquisition of knowledge and skills within traditional disciplines or develop transdisciplinary 21st century skills?
Employees versus employers	Do we want to develop students destined to be employees or employers?
Individual versus collaborative	Is *success*, in our context, an individual or collaborative endeavor?
Face to face versus distance	In the future, will students learn through face-to-face interactions or through online or distance-learning opportunities?
Diploma versus accumulated evidence of proficiency	Will student learning be authenticated through common graduation requirements (such as Carnegie Units) or through more personalized evidence of performance and accomplishment (such as digital portfolios, badges, modules, and so on)?
Stability versus innovation	Are we a district, school, or department that values stability and structure or innovation and risk?
Connected versus independent	Are we a district, school, or department that sees itself as part of a connected network or as an independent entity?

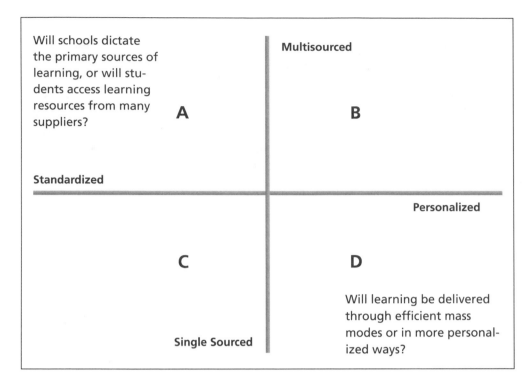

Figure 1.3: Sample four-quadrant chart.

Using this chart, we now have four potential futures to explore with many shades between them. Quadrant A represents a potential future where education is standardized and has diversified the sources and suppliers of learning; quadrant D represents a potential future where learning is highly personalized, but the sources and suppliers of learning are not as diverse and may be centralized; and so on.

Discussing Potential Futures

After graphing the polarities, we compare the potential futures and pick the most preferred from each chart by discussing the following questions: Where are we currently? What would each potential future look like? What are the benefits and drawbacks of each? Where do we want to be? Table 1.2 represents the questions and challenges associated with the potential future that each quadrant of figure 1.3 suggests.

Table 1.2: Questions and Challenges by Quadrant

Quadrant	Characteristics	Questions and Challenges
A **Standardized and Multisourced**	• Districts and schools can order state-adopted textbooks or resources from approved vendors. • There is some choice within a box-set environment. • School and class schedules are set. • Students are grouped by age.	• The approved resources may not support all teaching and learning approaches (such as inquiry). • There is minimal flexibility for schools and teachers regarding scheduling and grouping. • Would standardized testing increase?
B **Personalized and Multisourced**	• Learning resources would come from a wide variety of sources. • Students source much of their own learning. • Students assemble their own content (such as creating a playlist of learning like a musical playlist using programs like iTunes). • Teachers facilitate the process at an individual level. • Students meet in flexible groups. • Learning experiences take place anywhere and anytime (not necessarily in a brick-and-mortar schoolhouse).	• Who decides what quality is? • What are the criteria for success? • There is potential for an incoherent program (for instance, important skills can fall through the cracks). • How do we manage so many options? • How much autonomy and flexibility should we allow? • Are all students mature enough to handle this freedom? • How can we ensure accountability? • How would a student progress through the system (for instance, it could be a competency-based program)?

continued →

C **Standardized and Single Sourced**	• This future offers a guaranteed curriculum to all students. • There is centralized control over curriculum and learning resources. • Prescriptive syllabi ensure uniformity. • Inexperienced teachers can follow a script. • Rigid pacing guides keep everyone on track.	• Centralized structures can be bureaucratic. • A one-size-fits-all system discourages innovation and responsiveness to change. • How would we meet different learning needs, styles, and interests? • Rigid pacing guides encourage a coverage approach to teaching. • There is minimal flexibility for schools and teachers. • Standardized testing encourages excessive test prep.
D **Personalized and Single Sourced**	• There is centralized control of learning sources. • There is a guaranteed and coordinated curriculum. • Students select from a predetermined menu of sources and experiences. • Time frames and schedules can vary.	• There is freedom within structure. • How would we keep centralized materials up to date? • This future lends itself to a competency-based program. • A sophisticated database is necessary to manage the various pathways that students elect to take.

In a typical workshop, twenty to twenty-four sets of polarities will be mixed to create ten to twelve four-quadrant charts. The ensuing discussion will then result in the articulation of ten to twelve preferred futures from all of the potential ones. Once you graph and discuss various potential futures, do the following to summarize your work.

• Collect and collate the descriptions of all of the different future points described by the quadrants. Together, they form a rich description of preferred futures from varied perspectives.

- Schedule time for the group to reflect on its work and package it for communication to others. Generally, it is best to transfer the completed charts into a digital format, such as a simple set of PowerPoint slides, and collate the descriptions of preferred futures to bring them together in a single document.

When the descriptions of multiple preferred futures (each in the context of different mixtures of polarities) are synthesized, the result is a powerful vision for the desired future.

Facilitating the Generation of a Preferred Future

Scenario-based planning is not as complex as it may seem, but it does require skilled facilitation. Participants will find the process engaging and even fun if they are prepared and supported properly. Along the way, collaborative groups will often reach a number of powerful understandings and new perspectives that can yield one or more aha moments. Figure 1.4 presents a protocol for this process.

Process Phases	Planning Questions
1. Create small groups of four or five participants.	• How do we prepare groups for this sort of creative and collaborative process? • What mixture is beneficial within groups?
2. Give each group a poster-sized piece of paper with four quadrants that mixes polarities from different broad areas (for instance, one axis from technology and another from funding). Different groups should be given different mixtures of polarities.	• If not all polarities are within our control, how do we make sure that the mixture of polarities provides some eventual opening for planning and action? • What mixture of polarities provides the most powerful means to envision potential future scenarios?

Figure 1.4: A sample protocol for defining a preferred future.

continued →

Process Phases	Planning Questions
3. Have groups generate adjectives to describe each quadrant's representation of a potential future. This is the dialogue phase of the process. (Twenty to thirty minutes)	• If each quadrant represents a different potential future scenario, how would we describe these quickly and vividly? • What would people in these potential futures do? What would be the main characteristics of the environment? Where would control reside? Under what parameters would schools function? • How might the nature of school and learning be different within these potential futures?
4. Have groups discuss and agree on a desired end point for the department or organization. (Seven to ten years is an appropriate timeline.) This represents the ideal future relative to the polarities and potential futures. (Twenty to thirty minutes)	• Given that these quadrants represent a large variety of possible scenarios, which point represents the desired future scenario along each axis? • What is the right place to be in the future for our students? • What is the best possible point on the four-quadrant chart for the department or organization?
5. Have groups generate descriptions about this desired future.	Complete these sentences. • "This means that _____." • "What would we see if _____?" • "In this future, students will _____."
6. Groups can (and likely will) continue to describe where the department or organization is perceived to be now. This should be in relation to what we call drift points, which represent where the groups think the department or organization will end up in ten years relative to the trends and catalysts at play if it does not act. These can be powerful motivators and can bring some urgency to the work.	• Where are we now? • Where might we be in ten years if we do not act proactively in these areas? • What is our drift point?

Process Phases	Planning Questions
7. Groups should briefly share the results of their work with all participants to help identify similarities and tensions. (Ten to twenty minutes)	

The culmination of this collaborative process is an assessment of a group's current position and the identification of the desired future position. Achieving a group *aha!* is a very powerful phenomenon that can both consolidate and transform the group's thinking as it moves toward articulating its shared vision.

This process can be used at any level, from a small department to a large district with broad representation of stakeholder groups. For instance, Greg has worked with seventh-grade students who developed their own polarities and used the process to generate some powerful preferred futures for a simulated civilization-building project. They delved into polarity-driven questions, such as: Should basic services be universally available or provided through a user-pay system? Would such a system have a government that is an open democracy or one governed by a benevolent dictator who could get things done efficiently for the good of society? Through an exploration of various polarities and potential futures, the students developed keen insights, ideas, and compromises, all of which are key 21st century capacities.

Creating Futures-Oriented Artifacts

One of the first steps in moving from aspirational to intentional is to make your vision come alive for your community. A vision statement by itself is rarely compelling. In fact, such statements are too often filled with hollow clichés and are indistinguishable from one another.

The best way to bring a vision to life is to embed it within an accessible, invigorating narrative. People are drawn to stories, especially those that illustrate the abstract ideas and buzzwords contained in most visions. Your vision says that you want your students to become global citizens, but what does that mean? What would it look like? Your vision stresses the importance of developing 21st century competencies, but how would that differ from what students are doing in school now, and how will these competencies enhance opportunities for your students?

The narrative of your desired future can be portrayed in many ways. We want to show, not tell. We want to engage, not explain. A strong set of artifacts can bring your vision to life through the power of narrative.

So, what are futures-oriented artifacts? Simply put, they are tangible products that make the invisible visible. They serve to concretize an otherwise abstract vision. Here are a few examples.

- A student's journal entry describing a typical school day ten years from now, highlighting what he or she does on a daily basis and the ways in which he or she will learn

- An article that highlights a story important in this future

- A school schedule or timetable for a high school student in which the restrictive structures of traditional schedules have been removed

- A report card for an elementary student that gives a snapshot of the 21st century thinking and learning skills that will be part of future measures of success

- A student backpack full of the tools students will require to thrive in this new environment

- A digital portfolio of a student's work showing evidence of accomplishments on 21st century skills

- A teacher's job description and schedule that show the changing expectations for facilitators and mentors for learners

- A magazine cover or webpage that shows the headlines of the future

Developing a set of artifacts that represents your desired future of teaching and learning is an invigorating experience for all community members. It gives you a chance to engage in a hopeful future and be energized by what you see and create. Making these artifacts available at various meetings and events shows all involved what the vision looks like.

To begin this process, we suggest you do the following.

- The prior working group should collate and refine the output of the graphing process.

- The group should organize the descriptions of these preferred futures as primary-source materials for the generation of artifacts.

- The group should prepare a number of resources and raw materials (such as blank magazine covers and stock graphics, schedule templates, T-shirts, blank diplomas, and so on).

Do note that, again, participation depends on the context. If this is done at the department level, it need not be overly formal and will probably involve the participants of the scenario-building process. If this is done at the school or district level, a representative group should be drawn from a larger pool to help engage people in the emerging vision. Students should certainly participate in this process. Figure 1.5 presents a simple protocol to use in facilitating artifact development sessions.

Process Phases	Planning Questions
1. Ask members of the scenario-building group to share the preferred futures they developed. (Thirty minutes)	• What trends and catalysts did we engage with? • How did we come to understand the various potential futures represented by the four quadrants? • How did we choose our desired future from all of the potentials? • What did that desired future look like to us?
2. Introduce participants to the task and the materials at hand, and organize them into smaller groups (three to five people is generally good).	• How do we tell the story about a place and a time that don't exist yet? • What would people do in this new environment? • What would success look like for students and the organization? • What are the powerful stories, images, and headlines that might represent the real potential of that desired future?

Figure 1.5: A sample protocol for futures artifact development.

continued →

Process Phases	Planning Questions
3. Ask smaller groups to select artifact ideas from the menu provided (or devise their own) and get to work to develop a story of how each artifact reflects a possible future. (Sixty minutes)	• To whom are we communicating this story? • What is at the core of that story? • How might we show it—not just tell it? • How can we evoke strong, positive images in the audience's minds?
4. Bring everyone back together, and ask participants to show and explain their artifacts to the larger group. (Thirty to sixty minutes, depending on group size)	• In twenty-five words or fewer, what is your story? • What is the desired impact of your artifact? • Why did you choose that medium and that message? • How is your future story different from what we experience today?

Once you've completed this process, take the following actions.

• Gather all artifacts generated.

• Select a few strong and evocative artifacts from this session, and refine them.

• Send all outputs of the workshop to all participants in some form. This values the work and maintains engagement.

• Begin to publicly communicate refined artifacts through appropriate avenues. Introduce the artifacts to all community members at group events (such as assemblies, staff meetings, parent-teacher nights, and so on).

Figure 1.6 shows a few simple products from a futures-oriented artifacts workshop at Wesley College in Perth, Australia. Artifacts that participants developed included T-shirts, bumper stickers (on a real car bumper!), dioramas, songs, backpacks of the future, and many other tangible products of the visioning process.

Figure 1.6: Sample artifacts.

Artifacts serve to make things real, tangible, and exciting. The key is to creatively represent a vision of the future through multiple lenses that show its richness. People can rally around a story, especially if the student and stakeholder benefits are clear. Artifacts can become important tools in driving fear out of the change process and replacing it with positive feelings and hope.

Artifacts also represent a form of prototyping, which is a powerful way to test innovative ideas and future possibilities. In other words, artifacts can be used not only to inform people about a vision but also to offer concrete models of possibilities. They can help you gauge your community's reactions and help refine iterations of the vision.

Conclusion

In this chapter, we focused on ways of building a futures-oriented vision for your district, school, or department. While a vision of a preferred future can be largely intangible, the examples and processes presented here offer the potential to help people picture the future in positive and exciting ways. Once we have expanded our knowledge base and identified preferred futures that encompass our vision, the artifacts we create help concretize that vision and tell the story of that future.

While this may seem like a lot of work, it is vital to commit the time to help people co-construct a compelling and attainable vision of schooling. Shortcutting these early stages will dilute the goal clarity and commitment needed for the work ahead.

In chapter 2, we shift from these generative processes to articulating a mission and developing a plan to achieve it. To help that effort, we will introduce a major framework called Input-Output-Impact. We will also explore the development of a mission focused on key elements of student learning that represent the vision.

CHAPTER 2

From Vision
to Mission

How do we concretize our vision for modern learning into an actionable mission?

By acting on the ideas presented in chapter 1, you collaboratively developed an informed, futures-oriented vision for your organization. You also created a set of artifacts to help crystallize this vision. In this next stage, we move to transform your vision into a clear and achievable mission. In our experience, a lack of alignment between vision and mission creates a rudderless ship with little chance of achieving real improvement for students. Accordingly, articulating a firmly grounded and actionable mission is essential in achieving a vision for change at any level—district, school, or department.

Identifying Impacts

A vision can be thought of as what a district, school, or department *wants to become*. A mission can be thought of as its core business: what the district, school, or department *is about*. Our educational mission should thus serve to operationalize our vision. It should reflect the school's priorities in terms of the main outcomes of student learning based on the school's conception of its desired future. Unfortunately, mission statements often reflect a mixture of vague catchphrases and jargon. Consider the following examples.

- The XYZ School District believes that all students can learn and strives to help all learners reach their full potential.

- In the ABC School's social studies department, we nurture active citizens ready to succeed in a rapidly changing world.

Mission statements such as these are ambiguous and somewhat trite. They lack the specificity needed to guide actions. They leave us asking, "What does it mean for students to 'reach their full potential'?" "What would we expect an 'active citizen' to do?" "What do students need to 'succeed in a rapidly changing world,' and what does 'success' look like?"

Another common characteristic of poorly crafted mission statements is a focus on what the educational institution will provide for its students rather than on desired results in terms of student accomplishments. Here are examples.

- The EFG School is committed to providing a warm and nurturing environment in partnership with parents to support all of our learners.

- The QRS Independent School District offers a rigorous program of studies to prepare students for future success.

Such descriptions are well and good, but notice that being warm, nurturing, and rigorous are descriptions of *means*, not *ends*. Indeed, we find that organizations often confuse the environment, program, and facilities—all means for achieving a goal—with the goal itself.

How then do we move from a vision of a preferred future to an articulation of a mission that drives actions? Our recommendation is straightforward: an educational mission statement should state specifically the desired results in terms of student learning. In this book, we refer to these desired learning outcomes as *impacts*.

A simple definition of an *impact* is a desired student learning outcome that represents the aspirations of our vision and the core of our mission. More specifically, impacts have several distinguishing characteristics. They specify student learning outcomes that:

- Are **long term** in nature (they develop and deepen over time)

- Are **performance based** (they involve application by the learner)

- Involve **transfer** (application occurs in new situations)

- Call for **autonomous** performance from the learner (learning occurs without the teacher's coaching or prompting)

Schools can identify impact statements within traditional subject areas (disciplinary) as well as for outcomes that cross disciplines (transdisciplinary). In general, we expect to find disciplinary impacts rooted in departments' missions (for example, mathematics or visual art), while district- and school-level missions tend to feature transdisciplinary impacts, such as 21st century skills. Table 2.1 shows examples of both types.

Table 2.1: Two Types of Impacts

Disciplinary Impacts	Transdisciplinary Impacts
Effective writer	Critical thinker
Mathematical reasoner	Self-directed learner
Artist in multiple media	Collaborator

Operationally Defining Impacts

A critical step when working with transdisciplinary impacts is to reduce ambiguous terminology often associated with 21st century skills. People may have their own ideas as to what *creativity*, *innovation*, or *critical thinking* mean, and indeed, these concepts can be difficult to define. While there may never be universal definitions, it is essential that *your* school defines the impacts declared in *your* mission and communicates these clearly and consistently. Figure 2.1 (page 26) presents one school's approach to defining transdisciplinary impacts.

We must be talking about the same things in the same ways to clearly target and assess the impacts we profess to value.

Evaluating Impacts

In chapter 1, we described how to articulate a desired or preferred future through an exploration of various scenarios. We also outlined the process of creating artifacts of the future that will help ground this preferred future in the actual activities and environments that will characterize this future. These two elements,

Term: *Personal and social responsibility*		
Definition: Personal and social responsibility is defined and measured by growth and achievement in leadership, productivity, and self-direction. Students must be able to set and pursue personal, academic, family, and civic goals. They need the knowledge and skills to make good, ethical decisions; play an effective role in society at local, national, and global levels; become informed, thoughtful, and responsible citizens; and participate in the life of their schools, their community, and the wider world through service and volunteer opportunities.		
Leadership	**Productivity**	**Self-Direction**
Leadership is the capacity of an individual or team to guide, direct, or influence a group or institution in ways that bring about change and achieve stated purposes. Leaders in the 21st century must be adaptable, possess wide intellectual curiosity, and be lifelong learners. They must be willing to see value in different perspectives, be comfortable with uncertainty, and look globally for solutions and challenges.	Productivity involves prioritizing, planning, and managing for efficient and effective results through the use of real-world tools. The level of complexity often present in today's society requires workers—and students—to concentrate on the main goals of a project, carefully manage their work, and anticipate unforeseen events or possibilities. High productivity is a basic requirement for the typical 21st century knowledge worker.	Self-direction is the ability to set goals related to learning, plan for the achievement of those goals, independently manage time and effort, and assess the quality of learning and any products that result from the learning experience. Students who are able to learn independently and adapt in a world of rapid change will thrive in the 21st century.

Source: Catalina Foothills School District, Tucson, Arizona, 2008.

Figure 2.1: Sample operational definition of *personal and social responsibility*.

when combined, form the basis for the articulation of a few core impacts for your school. We can derive impacts from these raw materials by asking team members engaged in the prior tasks two simple questions.

1. What would a student be able to do in order to thrive in such a future?

2. What skills and aptitudes would he or she need to develop and utilize?

As participants consider these questions, we recommend that they propose impacts that meet three criteria:

To what degree does this proposed impact:

1. Reflect the highest goals of the organization, which are clearly linked to its mission?

2. Represent a desired transformation for learners?

3. Specify a long-term (exit-level) outcome stated in performance terms (such as *what learners can do*)?

The result should be a concise list of potential impacts that the group can present and discuss. In the end, the group can endorse a small number that represent the greatest convergence of perceived desired impacts. A school then moves from vision to mission by incorporating these specific impacts into mission statements. Here are a few examples of such mission statements for a school as well as for discipline areas.

The mission of GHI School is to develop learners who are independently able to:

- Become self-directed learners

- Apply critical thinking and ethical judgment when analyzing issues and taking actions

- Effectively communicate ideas for a variety of purposes and audiences using varied media

The mission of the mathematics department is to develop learners who are independently able to:

- Effectively use strategies and sound mathematical reasoning to tackle never-seen-before problems involving real-world and theoretical challenges

- Develop and critique arguments based on mathematical or statistical claims and evidence

The mission of the history department is to develop learners who are independently able to:

- Use knowledge of patterns in history to better understand the present and prepare for the future

- Critically appraise historical claims and analyze contemporary issues
- Participate as an active and civil citizen in a democratic society

As the examples suggest, impacts can target larger transdisciplinary goals—like those associated with 21st century learning—as well as academics. Notice that by highlighting desired impacts, these mission statements focus on specific student performances—*not* on the content that will be taught or what the organization will provide (such as a warm and nurturing environment, a fully stocked library, or tablets for every student). This distinction may seem academic, but it is critical and leads us to distinguishing impacts from inputs and outputs in order to support outcome-driven change backward through the entire organization.

Creating an Input-Output-Impact Framework

We have built this book around two interrelated planning frameworks: (1) Input-Output-Impact (IOI) and (2) backward design. Working together, they guide the movement from vision to mission to action. We'll describe the IOI framework here and explain backward design in chapter 3.

The IOI framework offers a simple but powerful mindset for focusing on the articulation of a vision and mission in terms of the important and measurable outcomes desired for students, teachers, and the community. When a school can articulate, clearly and simply, a set of targeted and compelling impacts, planning, implementing, and assessing progress take on a very different tone. Impacts allow us to focus on meaningful results that help sustain the school through the long and sometimes difficult journey toward the realization of its vision and the delivery of its mission. Thus, as a guide and as a strategic evaluation scaffold, the IOI framework allows schools to go from aspirational to intentional.

The IOI framework is essentially a way of focusing a school's resources and actions on the impacts articulated for the school. This focus is important and often missing in school-improvement planning and implementation. See figure 2.2 for the IOI framework.

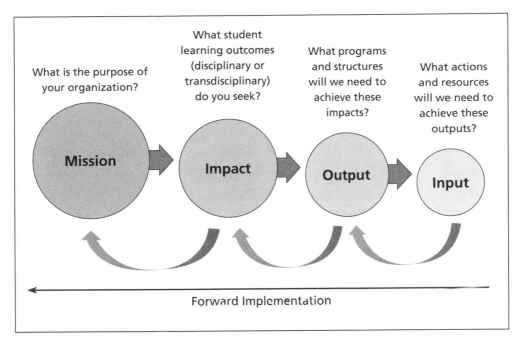

Figure 2.2: Input-Output-Impact framework.

The IOI framework and approach are deceptively simple, but they create complex ripples across the systems within a school. Maintaining an IOI framework can do the following.

- Help make the vision and mission focused on students and concerned with true transformation of individuals and the school

- Create a compelling common understanding of central goals for learning, which is key to engaging the community and developing support

- Elevate the school's transformational goals (impacts) and place them alongside more traditional ones (academic standards)

- Push change back through various teaching and learning systems and processes throughout the school (from desired impacts to actions in service of those impacts)

- Align processes across the school

- Ensure that a school's definition of success is anchored in student-learning impacts based on the mission

- Keep the school honest and focused through an ongoing inquiry into student learning as evidence of the achievement of impacts

While it may seem self-evident, the framework can be tricky to apply with fidelity, since its use often challenges comfortable habits and familiar ways of operating. We will be revisiting the IOI framework throughout this book and hope you will see how it can support positive change across your department or organization.

Figure 2.3 provides definitions, critical questions, and examples for each phase of the IOI framework in relation to service learning.

Phase	Definition	Critical Questions	Examples
Input	Resources (such as time or money), processes, programs, and actions directed toward mission	What actions, processes, and resource allocations will we need to move toward our vision?	• Establish curriculum-mapping committees within and across disciplines. Purchase electronic mapping software. • Provide schoolwide staff development on the Understanding by Design® framework for curriculum design. Purchase an electronic Understanding by Design unit planner. • Have district send out inquiries to local businesses and organizations regarding partnership possibilities. • Form a committee to explore service learning for students.

Phase	Definition	Critical Questions	Examples
Output	Tangible results of organizational inputs (such as curriculum or new structures)	What are the organizational results of our actions, processes, and resource allocations?	• Have teams develop curriculum maps for academic standards and 21st century skills. Review curriculum maps for vertical and horizontal alignment. • Teachers work in grade-level and department teams to develop Understanding by Design units. Review draft units against established criteria. • As a district, partner with several local businesses and organizations for student internships. • As a school, develop a series of structured service-learning opportunities for students.
Impact	Observable and measurable student learning based on mission	What are the most important observable and measurable goals for student learning relative to our mission?	• Students show increasing proficiency across the grades in 21st century skills areas. • Students show growth in understanding and transfer. • Students demonstrate specific skills and observable habits of mind valued in the workplace. • Students demonstrate traits of engaged citizens through their service experiences.

Figure 2.3: Sample definitions, critical questions, and examples of Input-Output-Impact for service learning.

Conclusion

In this chapter, we described ways to move your vision for a preferred future into a mission that can guide action. We introduced the Input-Output-Impact framework and highlighted the importance of focusing on student-learning impacts, both disciplinary and transdisciplinary, as the desired long-term outcomes of your mission.

We will now turn our attention to using backward design to begin that alignment process as we move from mission to action.

CHAPTER 3

From Mission to Action

How do we collaboratively plan backward from desired results to purposeful actions?

In the previous chapters, we concentrated on clarifying our destination in terms of lasting impacts. Now it's time to plan our journey. As we chart our route, we will move from desired impacts to identifying the specific outputs and inputs needed to realize our vision.

In this chapter, we will focus on unpacking transdisciplinary impacts—the overarching goals for student learning identified in a mission—via a method called *backward design*. While discipline teams can address traditional subject-area goals, working through transdisciplinary impacts requires a plan of action that cuts across subjects and grade levels, and backward design offers that deliberate action plan.

Backward Design

Essentially, backward design is a process to help you plan with the end in mind by clarifying your ideal result before trying to reach it. Grant Wiggins and Jay McTighe (2005, 2012) popularized the concept of backward design in their book *Understanding by Design*, in which they propose a three-stage process for the backward design of curriculum. Familiarizing ourselves with backward design in regard to curriculum will help us better use it in larger educational initiatives.

Curriculum Development

The idea of planning curriculum backward from desired results is certainly not new and can be summarized by a set of three essential questions for educators (DuFour, DuFour, & Eaker, 2008): (1) What do you want your students to learn? (2) How will you know they have learned it? and (3) What will you do to help them learn it? These questions summarize the intent and the sequence of the three stages of backward design described by Wiggins and McTighe (2005). Here is a brief summary of each stage.

1. **Identify desired results:** This first stage in the design process calls for clarity about long-term goals and instructional priorities. Teachers consider long-term goals based on established academic standards and related educational outcomes (such as 21st century skills). They identify the "big ideas" they want students to understand as well and frame companion essential questions around these targeted understandings. Finally, they identify more specific knowledge and skill objectives.

2. **Determine assessment evidence:** In stage 2, teachers are encouraged to think like assessors *before* planning lessons and activities in stage 3. This approach requires them to consider the assessment evidence needed to validate that they have achieved the learning outcomes targeted in stage 1. Doing so sharpens and focuses teaching.

3. **Plan learning experiences and instruction:** With clearly identified learning outcomes and appropriate assessment evidence in mind, teachers can now plan the most appropriate instructional activities for helping learners acquire targeted knowledge and skills, come to understand important ideas, and apply their learning in meaningful ways.

We have found that the intentional use of backward design for curriculum planning results in more clearly defined goals, more appropriate assessments, and more purposeful teaching. However, we have also observed that teachers do not always follow this approach when planning. Instead, there is a tendency on the part of some to jump from stage 1 to stage 3, to plan daily lessons and learning activities rather than consider long-term goals and assessment evidence up front. For these educators, backward design will require a shift in familiar planning practices.

Educational Initiatives

Backward design need not be limited to curriculum development. Indeed, we have found that it offers a robust process for organizational planning, and we recommend its explicit use when planning for *any* major educational initiative, including 21st century learning. In matters of school and district reformation (implementing a futures-oriented vision), the logic of backward design suggests the same three-stage process, with minor variations for overarching initiatives instead of curriculum.

Stage 1: Identify Desired Results

In this first stage, we establish the vision and long-term mission for 21st century learning in terms of impacts, such as specific student outcomes. We also consider what various constituents (teachers, parents, students, board members, the community, and so on) will need to understand about the proposed reforms, and we frame the initiative around essential questions to focus the efforts.

Stage 2: Determine Evidence of Success

In stage 2, we think like assessors *before* designing specific action plans. The backward design approach requires that we carefully consider the evidence we need to show that we are realizing our vision. As noted, evidence should primarily focus on impacts and not on inputs or outputs. Thus, backward design departs from the common practice of thinking about evaluation as something we do at the *end* of a project. We need clarity about the success indicators, which should be specified in terms of student performance. We need to get in the habit of asking the assessor's questions: "How will we know if we have achieved the desired results? What will we see if we are successful? What data do we need from the start to set a baseline in relation to our goals—to measure the gap between our goals and our current reality? How will we collect this evidence? How will we track our progress along the way?"

Such questions and their answers are key not only for making wise plans but also for clarifying an understanding of our mission and the chosen impacts on student learning. Only with clear and appropriate evidence in mind can we gauge our progress and know when we need to adjust our actions. Waiting until the end to see how (or *if*) they worked is simply too late.

In addition to impact evidence, we also gather evidence related to inputs and outputs—for example, the actions we take to achieve the desired impacts for student learning. These questions would be something like the following: What will we accept as evidence of staff understanding and proficiency? By what feedback system will we make timely adjustments to our plans to achieve our goals? What inputs may be needed to achieve our goals?

Stage 3: Develop the Action Plan

With clearly identified impacts and appropriate evidence in mind, it is now time to plan the actions needed to achieve our aims. Stage 3 is where traditional action planning occurs, via such questions as: What actions will we take? Over what time frame? Who is responsible for leading the various actions? What resources will we need to accomplish our goals? What professional development and support will be needed?

It is important to note that you should decide on the specifics—choices about tactics and actions, the sequence of activities, the deployment of resources, and so on—*after* identifying the desired results and specific evidence of impact. Just as we caution teachers against jumping to planning lessons and learning activities prematurely, enthusiastic leaders must also be careful not to jump to action planning before thoughtfully addressing the key questions of stages 1 and 2.

To recap, table 3.1 compares backward design for curriculum development and for educational initiatives. By grouping actions around larger, tangible products, we can better focus our actions around achievable results. In this way, the Input-Output-Impact framework for action planning is complete.

Table 3.1: Comparing Backward Design for Curriculum Development and for Educational Initiatives

	Curriculum Development	Educational Initiatives
Stage 1: Identify Desired Results		
Goals	Student learning outcomes for the unit	Larger impact outcomes for a district, school, or department
Understandings	Desired understandings for students to attain	The rationale and common understandings that various constituents will need in order to achieve impacts
Essential Questions	Central questions that will help drive student inquiry toward the targeted understandings	Central questions that build understanding among constituents and help focus implementation actions
Knowledge and Skills	Knowledge and skills students will need to acquire	Knowledge and skills—specified as part of action planning in stage 3—staff need to realize the promise of an initiative
Stage 2: Determine Evidence of Success		
Performance Tasks	Student demonstrations and performances that show evidence of attaining the targeted understandings, knowledge, and skill goals	Potential types and sources of impact evidence based on student performance
Other Evidence	Traditional assessments (tests, skill checks) that provide evidence of learning specific knowledge and skills	Evidence of the effectiveness of outcomes and inputs, such as the actions described in stage 3 of the implementation plan
Stage 3: Develop the Action Plan		
Action Plan	Learning activities that prepare students to provide appropriate evidence (stage 2) of attainment of the unit goals (stage 1)	Key actions and resources—divided into outputs and related inputs—needed to achieve the desired impacts

continued →

	Curriculum Development	Educational Initiatives
Stage 3: Develop the Action Plan		
Alignment	Alignment of all aspects of the unit plan	Alignment of the various educational and operational systems as necessary to achieve the impacts

A Backward Design Planning Template

In their book *Schooling by Design*, Wiggins and McTighe (2007) offer a backward design template to guide systemic planning. We have adapted the basic template to help unpack desired transdisciplinary impacts and guide the design of a sound implementation plan. Figure 3.1 presents the adapted backward design planning template with definitions and questions to consider for each element.

Stage 1: Identify Desired Results

Impacts

Impact goals specify the intended outcomes of schooling. These can include outcomes in academic areas (such as mathematics) as well as in transdisciplinary goal areas (such as self-directed learning).

Consider:

• What do future trends and drivers imply for education?

• What is our vision? Our mission?

• What specific impacts on student learning do we desire?

List impact goals here.

_____

_____

_____

_____

Understandings

These full-sentence statements identify what various constituent groups (teachers, parents, administrators, students, and policymakers) will need to understand about the future of schooling and the transformations needed to achieve it.

Consider:

- What is the importance of these impacts for students?

- What are our understandings about the changes needed to achieve them?

List understandings here.

_____

_____

_____

_____

Essential Questions

These open-ended questions are designed to engage various constituent groups in coming to a shared vision of our educational future and about the transformations needed to achieve it.

Consider:

- How might we develop a shared vision for future learning?

- What understandings and attitudes do various constituents need for our vision to be realized?

List essential questions here.

_____

_____

_____

_____

Stage 2: Determine Evidence of Success

Evidence of Impact

Specific evidence of student learning is based on the identified impacts.

Consider:

- What evidence of student learning and performance will count as evidence of success?

- What specific performance indicators and criteria will we use to evaluate student achievement of targeted impacts?

List evidence of impact here.

_____

_____

_____

_____

Sources of Evidence

These various assessments and other sources of evidence are needed to provide evidence of impact.

Consider:

- By what measures will we assess learning or performance?

- How will we obtain the needed evidence?

- How will we appropriately assess all impacts, not just those outcomes that are easiest to measure?

List sources of evidence here.

_____

_____

_____

Figure 3.1: Backward design planning template.

continued →

Other Evidence

Data on organizational inputs and outputs should also be collected from various sources of evidence.

Consider:

- By what measures will we gauge the effects of our short- and long-term actions and products?

- What feedback will we need to guide adjustments along the way?

List other evidence here.

_____

_____

_____

_____

Correlation to Inputs and Outputs

Various assessments and other sources of evidence are needed to evaluate inputs and outputs.

Consider:

- How will we collect needed evidence of effectiveness of our short- and long-term actions and products?

List correlation here.

_____

_____

_____

_____

Stage 3: Develop the Action Plan

Action Steps

Outlines of the major organizational actions are needed to attain the desired impacts. The action plan distinguishes between outputs (such as curriculum revisions and changes to report cards) and the various inputs needed (like training and allocation of resources).

Consider:

- What are the major programmatic and systemic changes (outputs) that we need to achieve, and how will we accomplish these when taking into consideration processes, time, and resources (inputs)?

List action steps here.

_____

_____

_____

_____

Outputs

Outputs are the specific products developed in pursuit of targeted impacts (curriculum revisions and changes to report cards).

Consider:

- What are the major structural pieces best suited to achieving this impact?
- What programs need to be put in place?
- What support is needed for these programs, such as professional learning, communication, physical space, and so on?

List outputs here.

_____

_____

_____

_____

Inputs

Inputs are the various organizational actions that will be undertaken and the resources needed to support them.

Consider:

- What are the steps or processes required to achieve the identified outputs?
- What actions will need to be taken and by whom?
- What resources might be needed to achieve these identified outputs?

List inputs here.

_____

_____

_____

_____

_____

Implications for Systems

Identify the ways in which various systems across the organization must work together in order to attain the desired impacts. It is important to consider these implications in the beginning so that each system can be integrated and aligned in achieving targeted impacts.

Consider:

- Are all systems properly aligned?
- Are any current systems out of sync or unsupportive of needed actions?
- What realignment might we need to achieve targeted impacts and support needed inputs and outputs?

Fill in the following rows with plans to keep all systems aligned.

Curriculum:

continued →

Assessment:
Instruction:
Grading:
Reporting:
Communication:
Professional learning:
Personnel (such as hiring, roles, and appraisal):
Schedules:
Resources:
Other:

Source: Adapted from Wiggins & McTighe, 2007.

As mentioned previously, the backward design approach can be used to develop an implementation plan for transdisciplinary, mission-driven impacts as well as for more traditional disciplinary outcomes.

A Sample Case Study: Developing Self-Directed Learners

We have observed that many schools and districts proclaim to be committed to developing self-directed learners. While the phrase may garner approving nods when included in a mission statement, one must ask to what extent the education program actually plans for the attainment of such an outcome. Consider how backward design might guide the intentional fleshing out of such an impact. Following is a stage-by-stage example of the process.

Stage 1

At the outset, it is important for all participants to understand the backward design process and be familiar with the modified *Schooling by Design* template. Typically, participants are educators and community members who have been involved in defining the futures-oriented vision and mission. Their understanding of how the transdisciplinary impacts were derived is important to the continuation of this process. We also recommend that a facilitator be identified to help guide the subsequent discussions. The facilitator may be a selected staff member or an external consultant. He or she will need to be familiar with the backward design process and experienced in facilitating small groups through structured tasks. The facilitator will need to prompt and focus the groups without overtly influencing the content developed.

We start with a direct, simple impact identified through the previous processes (see chapter 2): in this case, cultivating students who will be self-directed learners. Since such a goal can have different connotations, it is essential to clearly identify what it means in this school as well as why it is so important. We do this by identifying key understandings and essential questions that reflect the rationale for the goal. Articulating a set of understandings and essential questions is important not only for clarifying the impact but also for identifying the challenges, dilemmas, and investigations that need to take place in order to properly implement a plan to achieve the goal. These understandings and essential questions often provide helpful design parameters to guide important action steps.

Figure 3.2 (page 44) provides examples of possible understandings and essential questions for the impact goal of developing self-directed learners.

The process for completing stage 1 does not need to take a lot of time. Usually, a session of an hour or two will be enough to generate the initial understandings and essential questions that can be honed later. The test we use to know when we have generated a useful set of understandings and essential questions is simple: if someone were new to the process, would he or she come to understand the meaning, necessity, and richness of the impact by reading the understandings and essential questions?

Stage 1: Identify Desired Results
Impact Goal Students demonstrate the traits of self-directed learners.

Understandings	Essential Questions
• Self-directed learning requires a high level of metacognitive skills (such as goal setting, planning, and self-assessing) and dispositions (such as risk taking, persistence, and reflection).	• How might we cultivate the mindset needed for students to become self-directed learners?
• These metacognitive skills and habits of mind need to be taught and cultivated explicitly.	• How do we develop an appropriate continuum of the necessary skills and dispositions? • What tools will support the development of these skills?
• Learners can be supported in the development of these skills through the appropriate introduction of intentional tools and processes.	• What changes in instructional strategies, learning environments, and school structures will be necessary to make learning more personalized and self-directed?
• Students require a more personalized learning environment within which to develop effective self-direction.	• How do we assess and report on the development of the skills and habits of self-directed learning?

Figure 3.2: Examples of understandings and essential questions for developing self-directed learners.

Completing this stage of the process creates a strong set of shared agreements and understandings about what the goal means and why it is important. In generating essential questions, the group will have begun to dig into the important elements that need to be tackled as part of action planning and implementation. Stage 1 is important, as it is the foundation for later implementation.

Stage 2

Stage 2 asks groups to specify the types and sources of evidence that will show progress toward the chosen impact. Without clear measures directly linked to the desired impact, how would we know that we are achieving what we set out to do? While this may seem obvious, it is surprising how many districts and schools *think* they have succeeded at addressing targeted impacts by simply implementing a program, such as project-based learning. But where is the evidence that the program (the output of a great deal of input) has delivered on that particular goal? Simply doing something is not evidence of achieving a larger goal. A focus on evidence of impact and measures of success will help districts and schools avoid this mistake.

To identify types and sources of evidence, think about assessments already in place, especially for impacts in traditional subject areas. This step can prove more challenging when considering transdisciplinary impacts, however; while there may be opportunities for students to demonstrate these skills, few districts and schools have a system for consistently capturing evidence of transdisciplinary impacts. It's one thing to say that an impact goal is important and should be a target for development; it's quite another to press people to clarify exactly what we would accept as evidence that the student is demonstrating the desired impact. The matter is complicated further by the fact that collecting appropriate evidence of transdisciplinary impacts will most likely require new methods of assessment, record keeping, and reporting (elements we will explore in the coming chapters).

The group should also identify other potential sources of evidence that do not currently exist. This process allows participants to generate a rich palette of sources of evidence to guide future planning. Figure 3.3 (page 46) provides examples of possible sources of evidence for the impact goal of self-directed learning.

Stage 3

Stage 3 of backward design is where we develop an action plan to achieve the targeted transdisciplinary impacts. The good news is that much of the heavy lifting has already been done in stages 1 and 2. By identifying associated understandings and essential questions of developing self-directed learners, we have articulated key elements of curriculum design. By considering evidence and indicators of success and their sources, we have laid the groundwork for determining the needed assessments. Now, action planning becomes relatively simple. Working groups often feel relieved at this point, as the process becomes more linear and resembles more traditional planning processes.

Stage 2: Determine Evidence of Success

Evidence of Impact	Sources of Evidence
• Assessment of the use of learning management, metacognitive, and goal-setting tools	• Indicators and associated rubrics for metacognitive skills and dispositions
• Student demonstration of desired traits, aptitudes, and dispositions	• Lifelong learning skills and dispositions grafted onto appropriate performance-based tasks
• Results of individual goal setting	• Lifelong learning skills and dispositions grafted onto appropriate classroom assessments, noting that self-direction is necessary for success
• Student action plans developed through metacognitive reflections and external self-assessments (grit surveys, strength-finder tools, and so on)	• Goal-setting processes
• Student reflections on their development and teacher interpretation of those reflections in terms of desired traits and aptitudes	• Teacher, student, and peer use of indicators
	• Student self-reflection protocols with guides for teachers' interpretations
	• General academic performance

Other Evidence

• Improved performance in areas identified in goal-setting processes

• Engagement of students in providing evidence of progress toward developing self-directed learners

• Student, staff, and parent interviews and surveys

Figure 3.3: Examples of assessment evidence for developing self-directed learners.

Figure 3.4 presents examples of an initial action plan for the impact goal of developing self-directed learners. Note that we have identified key outputs and broken them down into related inputs.

For follow-up, planned outputs and inputs can be expanded into a more complete action plan. Let's break down the first major set of outputs and look at the associated steps and products for developing them (figure 3.5, page 49). The desire here is to create something that is teachable, learnable, and assessable from the impact. Without this level of detail, it would not be possible to implement this plan effectively, and we would remain at the aspirational level.

Stage 3: Develop the Action Plan	
Action Steps	
List the specific actions and sequence needed. Specify the person(s) responsible, due dates, needed resources, and other details to guide actions.	
Outputs	**Inputs**
Develop a clear set of foundational elements to allow for implementation within curriculum and assessment systems, including: • Operational definitions for key skills associated with lifelong learning • A set of developmentally appropriate performance indicators for lifelong learning skills • Overarching understandings and essential questions for lifelong learning skills	• Create working groups of school or district staff. • Have these working groups take part in a facilitated workshop to identify key skills. • Have groups identify appropriate performance indicators along a developmental continuum. • Collate draft work, and give it to constituent groups for feedback. • Have the working groups synthesize feedback and agree on a set of indicators for teachers to try.

Figure 3.4: Examples of inputs and outputs for developing self-directed learners.

continued →

Stage 3: Develop the Action Plan	
Outputs, cont.	**Inputs, cont.**
Identify key instructional approaches and structures needed to create a more self-directed learning environment, including: • Instructional approaches that best facilitate the development of lifelong learning skills • A collection of student tools to help in the explicit development of skills • A list of structural challenges and changes that would need to be adjusted (such as schedules, course structures, class groupings, reporting, and so on)	• Form a small group of teacher leaders as a research and development (R&D) group in this area. • Direct the R&D group to research and identify a set of initial approaches, including models that currently exist. • If available, have the R&D group propose site visits to schools that are explicitly targeting the development of self-directed learners and observe successful practices and lessons learned. • Direct the R&D group to research and gather examples of a potential set of student tools to support the skills. • Make sure the R&D group refines its list of approaches to identify high-leverage actions (those easiest to implement with the highest impact). • Allow the R&D group to propose instructional approaches to the administration for further action.

Implications for Systems

Too often, strategic plans will be developed for different systems within a school or district. For example, a school might have a five-year curriculum development plan, a three-year professional development plan, an annual school-improvement plan, departmental plans, and so on. We maintain that achieving the desired impacts *is* the focus of your overall strategic plan and that each system or department within the organization needs to understand its role in supporting the achievement of impact goals. Thus, a key output of the action-planning process should be the alignment of all systems to support the major impacts of the school's vision and mission. Figure 3.6 (page 50) shows potential implications for systems regarding the self-directed learning impact.

Outputs	Related Inputs	Resources	Responsible Party	Completion Date
• Operational definitions for key skills associated with lifelong learning • A set of developmentally appropriate performance indicators for lifelong learning skills • Overarching understandings and essential questions for lifelong learning skills	Create working groups by combining school- and district-level staff.	Release time for school staff as necessary ($X)	Curriculum leader	February 2015
	Have the working groups take part in a facilitated workshop to identify key skills.	Workshop facilitator ($X), release time for school staff as necessary ($X)	Facilitator	March 2015
	Split the larger groups into smaller working groups around small sets of skills.	Support materials and models, including printing and distribution ($X)	Curriculum leader	March 2015
	Have the working groups go through processes to identify appropriate indicators along a broad continuum of development.	None	Curriculum leader supporting group facilitators	May 2015
	Collate work, and give it to the larger working group.	None	Curriculum leader	May 2015
	Bring the larger group back together to discuss indicators developed and agree on a set to prototype with teachers.	Release time for school staff as necessary ($X)	Curriculum leader	June 2015

Figure 3.5: Example of action plan for developing self-directed learners.

Implications for Systems

- How might all departments contribute to achieving our mission?
- Are all systems aligned toward this goal?

Curriculum:

- Incorporate self-directed learning as part of unit goals, understandings, and essential questions.
- Adapt the curriculum-mapping system to allow for inclusion of self-directed learning skills across grades and courses.

Assessment:

- Analyze current assessments to identify potential areas for grafting self-directed learning skills.
- Develop and use performance indicators to regularly assess self-directed learning skills.

Instruction:

- Regularly employ the identified instructional approaches to cultivate self-directed learning skills.
- Identify gaps in instruction around self-directed learning skills, and plan to address these.
- Increase opportunities for students to develop and assess self-directed learning skills (such as more personalized learning).

Grading:

- Include performance indicators for self-directed learning as part of disaggregated grading.

Reporting:

- Include self-directed learning as part of reports of student learning.
- Address self-directed learning goals in parent conferences.

Communication:

- Develop and implement an ongoing communication plan for informing and educating parents and the community about self-directed learning.

Professional learning:

- Provide professional learning opportunities for teachers on instructional and assessment practices for self-directed learning.

Figure 3.6: Examples of systemic implications for developing self-directed learners.

Alignment Across All Stages

Beyond alignment across systems, the school must also align across stages. A key function of backward design (whether it be applied to curriculum design or toward districtwide impact goals) is such alignment. Sources of assessment evidence identified in stage 2 *must* be linked with the goals and understandings articulated in stage 1. Similarly, the proposed actions in stage 3 *must* systematically lead to the student performances desired in stage 2 and the goals targeted in stage 1.

An alignment check should always accompany such a process to ensure that all parts are mutually supportive. Here is a simple and efficient technique for checking the alignment of a curriculum plan *or* an initiative plan. After drafting a backward design plan, cover up your stage 1 goals, and only show the assessments and indicators in stage 2 (your plan to collect assessment evidence) to a colleague or a team. Then, ask members to tell you what they believe your goals (desired impacts) are based only on stage 2. If they can't guess your goals (or can only identify some of them), your targeted impacts and corresponding assessments are not yet tightly aligned. You can use the same technique with stage 3 by showing only your action plan and asking others to infer your stage 1 goals. This alignment check technique also helps people distinguish inputs and outputs from impacts.

Conclusion

We believe that change in schools is urgent. But we also believe that it must be staged properly and designed purposefully in order to focus our efforts to achieve important goals. A careful approach improves our chances of success. Thus, the backward design process described in this chapter helps us be more deliberate about our goals and the evidence of their success *before* jumping too quickly to action planning. Backward design also supports the alignment of all systems in support of our desired results. It is a "go slow to go fast" method that we have used successfully in a variety of educational environments. We trust that it will support your efforts in creating a system for modern learning.

In the next four chapters, we will examine critical systems related to identified impacts under the umbrella of backward design stages: curriculum (stage 1—identify desired results), assessment (stage 2—determine evidence of success), instruction (stage 3—develop the action plan), and reporting (implications for systems and alignment). IOI has been important to building an action plan focused on impacts and not simply inputs and outputs. The process of using backward design to align curriculum, assessment, instructional, and reporting systems with these desired impacts will drive the rest of the book.

CHAPTER 4

Curriculum for Modern Learning

What are the building blocks for 21st century curricula, and how do we develop them?

The Latin origin of the term *curriculum* translates roughly as "the course to be run." It is useful to think of a curriculum as the course or pathway to a destination. In education terms, the desired impacts on student learning—within traditional academic disciplines as well as transdisciplinary areas—define our destination. In this chapter, we will explore stage 1 of the backward design process: identifying desired results by discovering ways to operationalize your vision and mission, thereby establishing a comprehensive and aligned curriculum. To begin, let's take a look at the history of curriculum mapping.

Mapping 21st Century Curricula

Curriculum mapping is a well-established process for ensuring a coherent and vertically aligned curriculum across the grades. The idea came to prominence in the 1990s through Heidi Hayes Jacobs's work, and we have watched the process of curriculum mapping evolve since Jacobs's initial book was published in 1997.

The first generation of curriculum mapping asked teachers to generate *diary maps* to identify the unit topics and skills they taught. Teachers placed the unit topics and skills on a calendar map to show when they were taught and for how long. Then, grade-level or department teacher teams would meet to share their individual maps and look for gaps (for instance, "We found that no one is teaching how to write a research paper in high school English") as well as unproductive redundancies (for instance, "We learned that a unit on dinosaurs is being taught in kindergarten *and* grade 2"). This review and analysis of individual maps led to the development of consensus maps (Jacobs, 2004), whereby teams would agree on the overall curriculum content and sequence to ensure greater consistency across classrooms. Then, by reviewing grade and course maps in vertical teams, teachers were able to better align the curriculum across the grades.

The second generation of curriculum mapping emerged as states, provinces, and nations developed standards that teachers were expected to follow. While these standards are not a curriculum, per se, they do specify the knowledge and skills that students are expected to learn in the various grades and courses. Thus, mapping became a process of identifying the scope and sequence for the curriculum based on the established standards. In larger districts, curriculum committees rather than individual teachers at the school level often generated the standards-based curriculum maps by consensus. Some districts and schools went further, coupling the curriculum maps with pacing guides that specified the amount of time teachers should spend on the designated topics and skills.

The emergence of software mapping programs, such as Curriculum Mapper and Atlas Rubicon, provided educators with electronic tools for entering and storing the maps and enabled a variety of reports to check for alignment. Electronic mapping offers two important advantages over paper printouts in binders: (1) immediate access to the curriculum maps for teachers, administrators, and—when appropriate—parents and students and (2) the capacity for quick curriculum updating. Without easy access, curricula can become dormant; they end up as a collection of dusty binders that lack the clarity and direction they were intended to provide. A curriculum should be considered a living document and process, especially in a rapidly changing world with an ever-expanding knowledge base. Without the capacity to revise and update on the fly, curriculum documents become quickly dated.

The intent of second-generation curriculum mapping and pacing is curricular coherence and vertical alignment with standards. However, we have witnessed a problematic effect in some districts and schools—rigidly paced scope and sequence maps can unwittingly encourage a "coverage" approach to the teaching and testing of the discrete knowledge and skills listed on the maps. Moreover, since standards were developed primarily for traditional academic disciplines, the 21st century transdisciplinary goals are likely to fall through the cracks of conventional teaching and testing. (See Darling-Hammond, 2014; Jacobs, 2014a, 2014b, 2014c, 2014d.)

To avoid these potential problems, we propose a third generation of curriculum mapping as an alternative to a scope and sequence listing of discrete grade-level standards (knowledge and skills) in traditional subject areas. We recommend that a modern curriculum should be mapped backward from the long-term disciplinary and transdisciplinary impacts. More specifically, our maps need to shift from mapping inputs—the knowledge and skills we plan to teach—to the performances that will show the impacts we seek.

A Curriculum Blueprint

The owner of a construction company would never just deliver building materials to a job site and tell the workers to have at it. He or she would begin by consulting an architect who would develop a blueprint—a document that embodies the vision of the desired building and guides the subsequent construction. We think this approach applies to the construction of a curriculum for 21st century learning as well. Indeed, we need a vision to guide unit and lesson planning to ensure that student learning is coherent and connected within and across the grades. A curriculum blueprint is especially important to ensure that outcomes such as critical thinking and self-directed learning won't fall through the cracks during conventional subject-matter coverage.

Figure 4.1 (page 56) depicts our curriculum blueprint in two parts: (1) the "macro" curriculum that derives from our vision and mission to identify disciplinary and transdisciplinary impacts (transfer goals), overarching understandings and essential questions, and cornerstone tasks and (2) the "micro" curriculum enacted at the course, unit, and lesson levels.

Since we have already discussed the vision and mission processes, let's explore each of the elements in this curriculum blueprint, beginning with the long-term transfer goals.

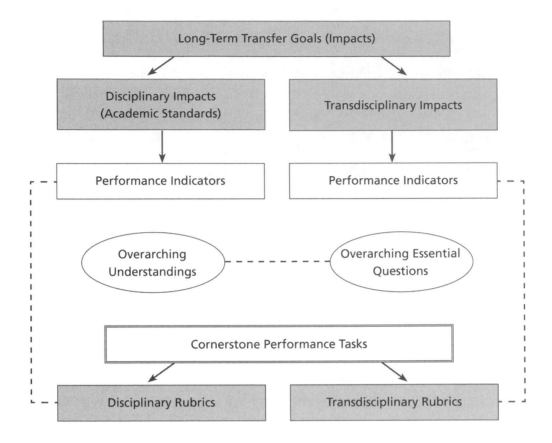

Figure 4.1: A curriculum blueprint.

Impacts as Transfer Goals

As discussed in chapter 2, the impacts we seek center on transfer—the ability for students to apply their learning in varied situations, not solely in the context in which they learned it. This capacity to transfer learning is crucial in an era in which new opportunities and challenges abound, even as much of the world's information can be googled on a smartphone. It is no longer sufficient for contemporary education to simply equip learners to give back existing knowledge. Thus, transfer goals highlight the effective applications of understanding, knowledge, and skill that we seek in the long run; they state what we want students to be able to do when they confront new challenges—both in and outside of school.

In *Education for Life and Work: Developing Transferable Knowledge and Skills in the 21st Century*, the National Research Council (2012) characterizes transfer goals as the essence of 21st century learning:

> We define "deeper learning" as the process through which an individual becomes capable of taking what was learned in one situation and applying it to new situations (i.e., transfer). Through deeper learning (which often involves shared learning and interactions with others in a community), the individual develops expertise in a particular domain of knowledge and/or performance. . . . The product of deeper learning is transferable knowledge, including content knowledge in a domain and knowledge of how, why, and when to apply this knowledge to answer questions and solve problems. We refer to this blend of both knowledge and skills as "21st century competencies." (p. 6)

Operationally, we propose that there are only a small number of truly long-term transfer impacts for each subject area and a few that cut across the disciplines. For example, a long-term impact in mathematics is for students to be able to tackle complex, real-world problems using sound mathematical reasoning. A long-term impact in history is for students to apply the lessons of history when considering contemporary issues. As we recommended in chapter 3, transdisciplinary impacts such as critical thinking should also be framed as impacts. For example, we seek to develop critical thinkers who do not simply believe everything they read, hear, or view. Rather, they should harbor an open-minded, yet skeptical, perspective. They should ask critical questions of the content and the source and seek alternative points of view.

A related characteristic of transfer is *autonomous* performance; essentially, learners need to be able to apply their learning independently, within and across subject areas. In the world beyond K–12 classrooms, no professor or boss is likely to hold your hand and direct your every action. Transfer goals call for a student to intelligently and effectively draw from a repertoire of skills, strategies, and tools to handle various challenges on his or her own.

Examples of transdisciplinary impacts are identified by the Partnership for 21st Century Skills (2009) as the 4Cs—(1) critical thinking, (2) creativity, (3) collaboration, and (4) communication—while examples of disciplinary impacts can be found in the Common Core State Standards (CCSS). The College and Career Readiness anchor standards for reading and writing (National Governors Association Center for Best Practices [NGA] & Council of Chief State School Officers [CCSSO], 2010a) specify the kinds of transfer performances that, by the end of K–12 schooling, students will need for success in higher education and the workplace. Here are two of these anchor standards (NGA & CCSSO, 2010a). Students should be able to:

- Read closely to determine what the text says explicitly and to make logical inferences from it; cite specific textual evidence when writing or speaking to support conclusions drawn from the text (CCRA.R.1)

- Write arguments to support claims in an analysis of substantive topics or texts, using valid reasoning and relevant and sufficient evidence (CCRA.W.1)

In sum, we propose that a small number of transfer impacts be identified within and across the disciplines and that these represent the impacts we seek in the long run. The curriculum is then mapped backward (grade 12–preK) from those desired impacts in order to chart the "course to be run" to achieve them.

Overarching Understandings and Essential Questions

Like the scaffolding on a building, overarching understandings and essential questions provide the intellectual *throughlines* to help the curriculum connect within and across grades and subjects in pursuit of the desired impacts. Think of understandings and essential questions as two sides of a coin. By engaging learners in exploring essential questions, we intend to develop and deepen their understanding of important ideas and processes.

In the macro curriculum blueprint, we refer to these elements as *overarching*, since the understandings are ones that develop and deepen over time. It is not expected that a learner will achieve these in a single unit or even a single year. Similarly, overarching essential questions are meant to be explored and revisited across the grades (compared to a topic-specific question that would only be considered within a single unit on that particular topic).

Overarching Understandings

If the capacity to transfer learning is a desired impact of 21st century schooling, then cultivating understanding is key. Rote learning of knowledge and skills is insufficient; one cannot apply learning to new situations if one does not have understanding. Accordingly, our curriculum blueprint calls for the development of understandings related to the identified transfer goals. We can pose this point as a question: What will students need to understand in order to effectively transfer their learning?

Understandings identify the important big ideas and processes that students should come to understand. They can differ in scope. While disciplinary understandings target the particular insights we want students to attain within a unit of study or a course, overarching understandings point beyond the specifics of a unit topic to the larger, transferrable ideas that spiral throughout the curriculum. Disciplinary understandings are more particular and less likely to transfer to other topics.

Understandings are identified for the purposes of:

- Focusing curriculum around enduring, transferable learning

- Encouraging active meaning making from students

- Enabling learners to transfer their learning to new situations

Good examples of overarching understandings can be found in the Next Generation Science Standards (NGSS Lead States, 2013). Known as *crosscutting concepts*, these ideas provide unifying conceptual strands that link across the specific topics, grades, and courses. Here is one example:

> *Cause and effect: Mechanism and explanation.* Events have causes, sometimes simple, sometimes multifaceted. A major activity of science is investigating and explaining causal relationships and the mechanisms by which they are mediated. Such mechanisms can then be tested across given contexts and used to predict and explain events in new contexts. (NGSS Lead States, 2013, p. 42)

Overarching Essential Questions

Essential questions are not meant to lead students to a prescribed answer, nor do they seek recall of factual information. They are meant to uncover important ideas and explore the nuances of process. In their book *Essential Questions: Opening Doors to Student Understanding*, McTighe and Wiggins (2013) characterize essential questions as follows. An essential question:

- Is open ended and typically will not have a single correct answer

- Should be intellectually engaging, intended to spark inquiry, higher-order thinking, discussion, and debate

- Points toward important, transferable ideas and processes within and across disciplines

- Raises new questions and sparks further inquiry

- Requires support and justification, not just an answer

- Recurs over time and is revisited over and over again

Like understandings, essential questions differ in scope and breadth. Overarching essential questions point beyond the particulars of a unit to larger, transferable ideas. They can fruitfully recur across the grades, spiraling throughout the curriculum to provide conceptual links within, and sometimes across, disciplines. Disciplinary essential questions are more specific. They guide the exploration of ideas and processes around *particular* topics within a unit or course.

Figure 4.2 presents examples of overarching understandings and overarching essential questions linked to corresponding transfer goals—three in academic subject areas and two for transdisciplinary impacts.

Impacts	Transfer Goals Students will independently …	Overarching Understandings	Overarching Essential Questions
Disciplinary Examples			
Language Arts	Comprehend a variety of texts	Effective readers employ appropriate strategies based on the content and their purpose for reading.	• What do effective readers do? • How does what you read influence how you should read it?

Impacts	Transfer Goals Students will independently . . .	Overarching Understandings	Overarching Essential Questions
Mathematics	Use mathematical modeling for descriptive and predictive purposes	Mathematicians create models to interpret and predict the behavior of real-world phenomena. Mathematical models have limits and sometimes distort or misrepresent data.	• What is the best way to model this phenomenon? • What are the limits of mathematical modeling and representation?
Visual Arts	Use various visual media to express ideas and feelings for various purposes and audiences	Visual artists choose to follow or break established conventions in pursuit of expressive goals.	• What style and medium should I use to express my ideas and feelings? • Why and when should an artist depart from established conventions?
Transdisciplinary Examples			
Critical Thinking	Critically appraise information and claims, ask critical questions, and deliberately seek differing points of view before reaching a conclusion	A critical thinker does not simply believe whatever he or she reads, hears, or views. He or she remains skeptical, asks critical questions, and seeks alternative points of view.	• How do I know what to believe in what I read, hear, or see? • Is this a credible and unbiased source? • What other perspectives should I consider?

Figure 4.2: Sample overarching understandings and essential questions.

continued →

Impacts	Transfer Goals Students will independently …	Overarching Understandings	Overarching Essential Questions
Self-Directed Learning	Set goals and pursue them independently, self-assess and adjust, and seek feedback to improve their learning and performance	A self-directed learner sets goals and pursues them independently. He or she regularly self-assesses and seeks feedback to improve learning and performance.	• What do I want to learn or achieve? • How am I doing? • How can I improve my learning or performance?

In sum, overarching understandings and essential questions provide the guide-posts for helping educators construct a curriculum that spirals around a set of recurring ideas and processes within and across subject areas. These overarching elements provide the intellectual throughlines needed for a curriculum to be coherent and directed toward long-term transfer—the desired disciplinary and transdisciplinary impacts. By framing a curriculum in this way, we intend to develop and deepen students' understandings and support their capacity to apply their learning on their own in new circumstances.

Overarching Understandings and Essential Questions for Disciplinary Impacts

At the International School of Beijing, Greg facilitated working sessions to articulate disciplinary long-term transfer goals and a set of associated overarching understandings and essential questions. These sessions brought together teacher leaders from the early years through grade 12 for each curriculum area to engage in collaborative discussions about these foundational elements. The process was positive, focused, and productive, resulting in sets of draft transfer goals, under-standings, and essential questions in a relatively short period of time for each curriculum area. Nearly all participants commented on the benefit of working collaboratively with teachers from other divisions. Figure 4.3 presents an example of science disciplinary impacts with the associated overarching understandings and essential questions.

Transfer Goals Students will independently . . .	Overarching Understandings	Overarching Essential Questions
Use scientific approaches and methodologies to investigate phenomena, claims, results, and information	Science is a disciplined way of thinking about and systematically investigating the world in which we live.	• What can or should we question? • How do we investigate this? • What does this mean, and is it true? • How do I turn information into understanding? • How do I communicate what I have learned through scientific investigation?
Use scientific thinking to understand the relationships and complexities of the world around them	Scientific thinking recognizes that all things are part of interrelated systems.	• How are things related? • How do you recognize a system? • How does a system achieve or maintain balance? • What patterns exist in systems?
Identify real-world dilemmas and opportunities and apply scientific thinking to develop solutions for them	Through curiosity, scientists innovate, solve problems, and sometimes create new ones.	• Why be curious? • What is the problem or need? • What do I need to know and understand about this? • Where do science and innovation meet? • Is this the best solution? • What is the impact?

Figure 4.3: Sample macro curriculum elements for disciplinary impacts in science.

Once these elements were drafted, the teachers in the working groups took the long-term transfer goals back to their colleagues for feedback and suggestions. The response was largely positive because of the collaborative nature of the process and due to the fact that these long-term transfer goals resonated with teachers since they reflected the heart of their disciplines.

Once teams finalized the sets of overarching essential questions in each discipline, the school printed attractive posters for displaying them. Figure 4.4 shows a mathematics example.

The school prominently placed the posters in classrooms, hallways, and the faculty room. Such public placement highlighted the idea that the curriculum spirals around a recurring set of important questions and encouraged staff and students to keep considering these questions across the grades.

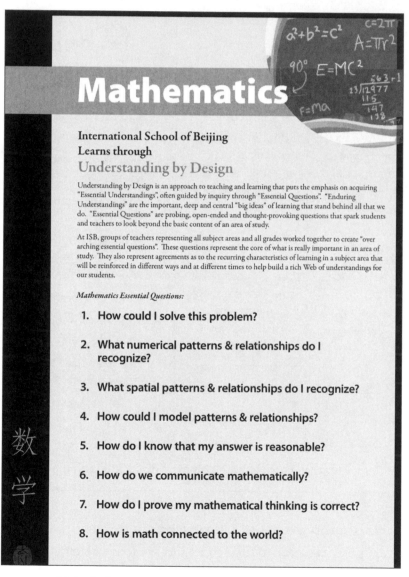

Source: International School of Beijing, 2010. Used with permission.

Figure 4.4: Poster showing overarching essential questions for mathematics.

Overarching Understandings and Essential Questions for Transdisciplinary Impacts

Once you've identified transdisciplinary impacts and operational definitions for them (see figure 2.1, page 26), we recommend developing a small set of associated overarching understandings and essential questions for these transdisciplinary impacts, as discussed with disciplinary impacts previously. Figure 4.5 (page 66) presents examples for one such impact—*global citizenship.*

Cornerstone Tasks

Cornerstone tasks are a key element in our curriculum blueprint. Cornerstone tasks are curriculum-embedded performance tasks that engage students in applying their knowledge and skills in an authentic context. To invoke the construction analogy again, we can think of these tasks as a cornerstone on a building; they serve to anchor the curriculum around the most important performances that we want learners to be able to do on their own with acquired content knowledge and skills. In short, cornerstone tasks operationalize the long-term transfer goals—the desired impacts of a curriculum. Moreover, we have found that such performance tasks serve as *the* practical vehicle for integrating the transdisciplinary impacts with academic subject matter.

In the next chapter, we will describe cornerstone tasks in more detail and offer a process for developing them.

Conclusion

Once we know where we need to end up, we can figure out how to get there. A focus on impacts suggests that we *first* map out the cornerstone assessment tasks that will provide evidence of desired impacts—transfer of learning. Then, we map out the overarching understandings that students will need in order to transfer their learning and the associated essential questions that will spiral across the grades. Finally, we can place specific course and unit designations on the maps. In this conception of curriculum mapping, the knowledge and skills are considered inputs—the enabling skills students need in order to complete tasks (outputs) that demonstrate their capacity to transfer their learning to new, authentic situations.

Transdisciplinary Impact	Transfer Goal Students will independently ...	Overarching Understandings	Overarching Essential Questions
Global Citizenship	Take ethical, constructive actions in an interdependent world by applying global understandings and thinking strategies	We live in an interrelated world. We relate to and understand one another across cultures and circumstances. We make many decisions that have impacts, intended and unintended, within a complex and ever-changing world.	• What makes us different or the same? • Why don't we all see things the same way? • How do my decisions and actions affect others? • How are things connected? • Why care?

Figure 4.5: Sample curriculum elements for a transdisciplinary impact: *global citizenship*.

Mapping the curriculum in this manner will make it more likely that mission-related, 21st century skills will be naturally and appropriately fused with the teaching and assessment of academic standards. Ultimately, a modern curriculum should reflect our mission of preparing students to apply their learning to the unpredictable opportunities and challenges they will face.

In this chapter, we described how to use backward design to create a curriculum blueprint, which is a framework for designing a curriculum that honors the mission of 21st century learning. In the next chapter, we will explore the use of cornerstone tasks as a vehicle for fusing 21st century skills with traditional content and will provide evidence of student progress toward targeted impacts.

CHAPTER 5

An Assessment System
for Modern Learning

How do we assess both disciplinary and transdisciplinary achievements?

Consider trying this interesting and revealing action research process. Collect samples of the assessments that teachers in your school or district are currently using as the basis for evaluation and grading. Then present these to a panel of outsiders for review (such as educators from another school or district, parents, or community members), and ask them to tell you what they think your mission and desired impacts are, given what is being assessed. Do they see evidence that transfer of learning is valued or that transdisciplinary impacts and 21st century skills are priorities? Indeed, it is often the case that observers will detect a mismatch between stated impacts and the commonly used assessments. This action research process sheds light on a fundamental idea of backward design—that our assessments should closely align to our desired impacts. In other words, what we assess signals what we value. If we don't assess it, then students are likely to see it as unimportant and won't take it seriously.

In this chapter, we will explore the type of assessment system needed to align with your mission. We'll begin by examining principles and goals of effective assessment of student learning and then look at a framework for planning these assessments. We'll drill down for a more focused look at the performance areas and indicators that make up transdisciplinary impacts and introduce the idea of grafting these impacts onto cornerstone tasks. Finally, we will offer suggestions for mapping cornerstone tasks and creating rubrics in order to regularly review student performance.

Principles of Effective Assessment

Schools should engage relevant members in discussions of common principles and assessment and avoid simply adopting a set of canned principles. This is a situation where the input is as important as the output. We've often observed that foundational elements of a school's blueprint (such as assessment principles) that have been copied and pasted—rather than arrived at through dialogue and discussion—are not effective. Thus, it is our contention that dialogue and a set of underlying principles should guide the design and implementation of assessments at the classroom, school, and district levels. Jay offers five principles of effective assessment in his ebook *Core Learning: Assessing What Matters Most* (McTighe, 2013) and in *Integrating Differentiated Instruction and Understanding by Design* (Tomlinson & McTighe, 2006), which we summarize here.

1. **Assessments should serve learning:** A fundamental purpose of educational assessment is to inform teaching and improve learning. This principle suggests that assessment is a feedback system to provide teachers *and* students with helpful information in order to enhance their performance. Assessment practices that support learning have well-known characteristics; they feature clear goals, authentic applications of knowledge rather than merely testing for factual recall, known criteria and models of excellence, ongoing feedback, opportunities for learners to retry and revise, more than one way to demonstrate learning, and learner self-assessment and goal setting. Of course, assessments also serve an evaluation and grading function, but this purpose should not come at the expense of learning.

2. **Multiple measures provide a richer picture:** Assessment is a process by which educators make inferences about what students know, understand, and can do based on information obtained through assessments. Our inferences are more dependable when we

consider various sources of evidence, since all forms of assessment are susceptible to measurement error. Consider a photographic metaphor. A photo album typically contains many pictures taken over time in various settings. Thus, the album presents a more accurate and revealing portrait of an individual than does any single snapshot. Likewise, with educational assessments, we will obtain a truer representation of student learning and growth by reviewing multiple pictures rather than a single snapshot.

3. **Assessments should align with goals:** The logic of backward design demands that our assessments be well aligned to our goals. Educators often refer to the validity and reliability of an assessment. However, a more precise conception has to do with the extent to which the results of an assessment permit valid and reliable *inferences*. For any assessment to allow valid inferences to be drawn from the results, that assessment must provide an appropriate measure of its targeted goals. Since we have different types of goals (knowledge, skills, understandings, transfer, habits of mind, 21st century skills, and so on), we need a variety of assessments to provide proper evidence of their attainment. To extend the photographic metaphor, we would expect different types of pictures in our assessment photo album. For instance, we could use a multiple-choice test to see if students have learned important factual information, a written explanation to assess their understanding of a concept, and a performance task to see if students can transfer their learning to a new situation.

4. **Assessments should measure what matters:** Assessment principles 3 and 4 get at the heart of this book. Given our attention to a clear and compelling vision for future learning and an articulated mission to guide our actions, it is essential that we assess *all* of the impacts we envision, not just those traditional academic objectives that are easiest to test and grade. The old adages apply here: "We measure what we value," "What gets measured is what gets done," and "It only counts if it counts." If we say we want students to be able to transfer their learning to new situations, then we need assessments that call for transfer in authentic situations. If we proclaim to be

developing self-directed learners, then we need evidence of the growth of this capacity over time. Since most mission-related impacts, such as the 4Cs, do not lend themselves to a moment-in-time test, we will need to think about a collection of evidence obtained over time to gauge students' performance and growth in these valued areas.

5. **Assessments should be fair:** The principle of fairness in assessment simply means that we must give all students an equal chance to show what they know, understand, and can do. Standardized tests claim to be fair since the conditions for administering the test, such as strict time limits and uniform scoring procedures, are meant to ensure that all students are assessed in an identical manner. Despite their benefits, standardized assessments have a downside, namely that learners differ in their knowledge and skill levels and in their preferred modes for demonstrating their learning. Thus, a one-size-fits-all approach to assessment may not, in fact, always be fair or appropriate. Since teachers are less constrained by the technical demands of large-scale testing, they have greater flexibility in allowing students to demonstrate their learning and performance in varied ways. For example, an English learner might be allowed to show her understanding of a science concept visually or by an oral explanation rather than through multiple-choice test items that she cannot read. In some cases, it may be appropriate to allow certain students more time to complete a task, especially when competency is the goal rather than speed.

Appendix D (page 169) includes examples of assessment principles developed collaboratively at the school level.

Before creating appropriate educational assessments, however, we must first consider the various types of goals available, since the goal will dictate the type of assessment to use.

Types of Goals

McTighe (2013) describes five interrelated but different goal types for learning. The differences are noteworthy, since their development requires different approaches to both assessment and instruction. Here is a summary of the five goal types and their implications for assessment.

1. **Knowledge:** Knowledge goals specify what we want students to know, such as facts (the capital cities of countries or chemical symbols) and basic concepts (different shapes).

   Assessment implications: Evidence of attainment of knowledge goals can be determined through objective test or quiz items or through teacher questioning. Typically, knowledge goals have a correct answer, so evaluation is binary—either correct or incorrect. This factor enables machine scoring of selected-response test items, a format used widely on standardized tests as well as in classroom assessments.

2. **Skills and processes:** These goals are procedural in nature and identify what students should be able to do. Skills involve discrete behaviors (buttoning a shirt or hitting a ball with a bat), while processes involve more complex actions requiring multiple steps (extended writing or scientific investigation). Processes involve a set of composite skills.

   Assessment implications: The most appropriate assessment of skills and processes calls for the learner to perform in order to demonstrate his or her competence. Teachers or assessors then use direct observation or an examination of a product or performance (a writing sample) to gauge proficiency. Unlike assessment of knowledge for which there is usually a single correct answer, the assessment of skills and processes can best be conceived as a continuum of proficiency levels from novice to expert, similar to different colored belts in karate.

3. **Understanding:** Understanding goals refer to the big ideas that we want students to comprehend at a deep level. Such ideas are conceptual and inherently abstract, such as adaptation or the awareness that form follows function. Good examples of understanding-based goals may be seen in the crosscutting concepts of the Next Generation Science Standards—

Scale, proportion, and quantity: In considering phenomena, it is critical to recognize what is relevant at different measures of size, time, and energy and to recognize how changes in scale, proportion, or quantity affect a system's structure or performance. (NGSS Lead States, 2013)

Assessment implications: The most appropriate assessments of understanding ask students to do two things: (1) *apply* their learning to a new situation and (2) *explain* or defend their answer and their process for arriving at it. Thus, we advocate the use of performance assessments that require application (ideally in an authentic context) with explanation (show your work, justify your conclusion, and cite text evidence to support your interpretation).

4. **Disposition:** Also called *habits of mind*, these disposition goals characterize productive ways of thinking and acting—in school and in life. The Common Core's Standards for Mathematical Practice include dispositions by noting that mathematically proficient students "make sense of problems and persevere in solving them" (NGA & CCSSO, 2010b). Arthur Costa and Bena Kallick (2008) identify sixteen habits of mind that parents, teachers, and employers recognize as valuable. Their set includes listening with understanding and empathy, thinking flexibly, striving for accuracy and clarity, managing impulsivity, remaining open to continuous learning, and thinking about thinking (metacognition). Dispositions are inherently transdisciplinary in nature; they apply within and across subject areas and throughout life.

   Assessment implications: While we might give a test or quiz to see if students have learned basic facts, an on-demand assessment of dispositions would be unnatural and inappropriate. Can you imagine scheduling a test on open-mindedness? Assessing dispositions is best accomplished through a collected-evidence model of observations and student self-assessments, based on defined performance indicators, that are gathered over time.

5. **Transfer:** A transfer goal highlights the effective application of knowledge, skills, understanding, and disposition. Transfer goals state what we want students to be able to do with their learning

when they confront new challenges outside of school. These goals have three distinguishing characteristics. First, they stipulate *long-term* performances or exit goals toward which teachers collectively work across grade levels. Second, transfer goals demand *transfer*; learners must be able to apply their learning in new and unpredictable circumstances. The third characteristic is *autonomy*; the learner is expected to be able to perform independently without excessive guidance or scaffolding.

Assessment implications: We think that assessing transfer should be obvious—we need to collect evidence of students' growing abilities to apply (transfer) their learning to increasingly authentic and complex situations and do so with increasing autonomy. We propose to do this through a set of recurring cornerstone tasks mapped out across the grades. We will describe these in greater detail shortly.

We propose that educators identify a small number of long-term transfer impacts—the kinds of performance capabilities we wish to cultivate over time. In order to assess these impacts, we'll need to further define them in terms of performance areas and performance indicators.

Performance Areas and Performance Indicators

Frequently, schools identify transdisciplinary impacts within their visions and missions, but—unlike disciplinary impacts (academic standards)—they rarely unwrap these into performance indicators that are demonstrable, learnable, and teachable. Without this level of definition, these larger goals often remain aspirational. It is essential that this process be undertaken early so that the school's goals are clear and the school's definition of *success* can be integrated into curriculum design, assessment processes, practices, and in the end, the reporting of students' accomplishments and growth.

Once you have identified your transdisciplinary impact and identified overarching understandings and essential questions—as discussed in chapter 4—we recommend breaking the impact down further into performance areas and performance indicators (figure 5.1, page 74). Unpacking the impact down to performance indicators is very important, since these specify what students will do to provide developmentally appropriate evidence of performance and growth over time. As such, performance indicators are critical for assessment because they point out the particulars to look for when evaluating student performance.

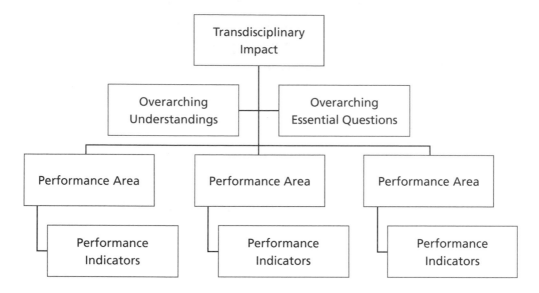

Figure 5.1: Unpacking the layers of a transdisciplinary impact.

You may recognize that such a structure is similar to the way in which disciplines are often broken down into strands and benchmarks.

We'll focus on unpacking the transdisciplinary impact of *self-directed learning* into usable performance areas (figure 5.2). First, we list the overarching understandings and essential questions using the process learned in chapter 4. Then, we brainstorm the performance areas related to the impact.

The delineation regarding what self-directed learners *are*—the performance areas—is important, but we still need to know what they *do* in order to recognize and assess demonstrations of these skills and traits. Thus, we need to brainstorm performance indicators.

Unpacking transdisciplinary impacts into performance indicators is a relatively simple process that helps groups more clearly define these sometimes slippery mission- and vision-driven elements. It is important to note—and ensure team members understand—that this process is not designed to bring about a comprehensive, polished, perfect list of indicators. Rather, it is designed to spark thinking about exactly what a student would do to show evidence of growth and attainment of a desired impact. This can seem like a daunting task, but there are many sources that provide good examples as starting points for unpacking 21st century skills. We include a bank of such examples in appendix B (page 149).

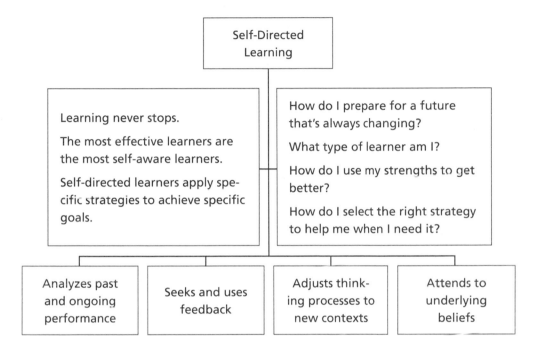

Figure 5.2: Sample performance areas.

Once you've brainstormed performance indicators, organize them along a developmental continuum to guide a common understanding of the types of demonstrations appropriate for different grade bands. It's obvious that a single set of a few performance indicators is not enough to provide guidance on the skills and aptitudes we want students to develop and demonstrate across the developmental spectrum, so creating a continuum will help us see what we are building *from* and *toward*.

Developmental continua are often used in areas such as reading and writing development. They are also well suited to helping chart the desired growth progression for students in regard to transdisciplinary impacts. Figure 5.3 (page 76) provides a small sample of performance indicators unpacked from figure 5.2. This is not presented as a definitive or complete list but merely as an example of the final level of unpacking.

Impact: Self-Directed Learners		
Performance Area: Showing Self-Awareness		
Elementary School Performance Indicators	**Middle School Performance Indicators**	**High School Performance Indicators**
• Demonstrating active engagement in learning • Demonstrating increased self-confidence as a learner through the application of strategies • Recognizing personal strengths and limits regarding memory and other cognitive tasks • Sustaining focus on task, goals, and planned processes	• Articulating a sense of accomplishment and personal self-satisfaction in his or her work • Demonstrating self-direction in learning tasks • Identifying as a learner able to be successful in the face of challenges • Demonstrating motivation to learn a metacognitive strategy as a means of success • Affirming ongoing processes verbally	• Demonstrating a high level of self-efficacy as a learner • Approaching challenges as opportunities to grow as a learner • Demonstrating intrinsic motivation • Being determined to improve abilities as a learner in the completion of all tasks and challenges

Figure 5.3: Sample performance indicators.

You can use the unpacking process for any transdisciplinary impacts embedded in your district, school, or department mission.

Figure 5.4 presents a protocol Greg used with teacher teams at the International School of Beijing to organize performance indicators along a continuum.

Actions to take before this process:

1. Overarching essential understandings and essential questions should have been developed through the earlier articulation of transdisciplinary impacts.

2. Gather examples of rubrics or descriptors for your transdisciplinary impact from various sources. There are many resources available through a simple web search.

3. Distribute these to the unpacking team.

4. Ask team members to skim over them before the workshop, noting any themes, trends, essential understandings, or essential questions.

5. Print examples, and cut sample performance indicators into individual slips of paper.

6. Keep a list of sources so that these can be properly referenced with the finished product.

7. Prepare a large piece of butcher or poster paper as a continuum by dividing it into a simple, large grid with grade levels for the column headers and space to write the performance indicators in the rows.

Note: Small teams should undertake this process (four or five people per transdisciplinary impact). It is a great process for teams of teachers, but administrators should also take part, thereby sharing in the understandings and product developed. You may also decide to include students and parents in the process.

Process Phases	Planning Questions
1. The team meets to discuss essential understandings and essential questions developed from early articulation of the impact. (Ten to fifteen minutes)	• What do these overarching elements tell us about the doing of this impact? • What key elements are both explicit and implicit? • How do we uncover the richness of the impact through our unpacking of it?
2. The team first breaks the impact down into an initial set of a few (two to five) major performance areas. (Thirty to forty-five minutes)	• What are the major characteristics of a person who demonstrates this impact? • What major performance areas are part of demonstrating the impact? • Can students at all developmental stages engage with this performance area at an appropriate level?

Figure 5.4: A protocol for organizing performance indicators on a continuum.

continued →

Process Phases	Planning Questions
3. Lay out the large sheet of butcher or poster paper on a central table. Add the performance areas generated in the previous step to the row headings. Distribute the sample performance indicators to team members along with glue sticks. Ask team members to take a few indicators and place them appropriately on the butcher paper grid (aligned with the appropriate performance area and developmental stage or division). This should be a quick alignment exercise and not drawn out to create a perfect product at this stage. (Twenty-five minutes)	• How do specific performance indicators fit within the identified performance areas? • At what developmental stage could you visualize a student demonstrating this indicator?
4. Team members discuss the developing continuum, paying special attention to the grouping of similar indicators, horizontal flow, whether a student can demonstrate an indicator and a teacher can capture it, and so on. (Twenty to thirty minutes)	• Is there a flow across school levels or developmental stages for each performance area (horizontal)? • Is there a flow across all of the performance indicators for school levels or developmental stages (vertical)?
5. Team members adapt the sample indicators as they see fit. They can write new ones on sticky notes to fill gaps and place them in the desired spots on the continuum. (Twenty to thirty minutes)	• If the flow across school levels is choppy, how might we bridge those gaps or developmental stages?
6. Team members discuss the output, making minor tweaks until they believe the output is OK for prototyping and feedback. (Twenty minutes)	• How can teachers and students use the performance indicators to gain clarity about this output? • Will the performance indicators support the development of this output?

> Actions to take after this process:
>
> 1. Collect the butcher or poster paper, and recreate it in digital form for distribution.
> 2. Schedule a time for the team to come together at a later date to reflect on its work and discuss communication and prototyping plans.
> 3. Present the list of performance indicators as *working drafts* for feedback from the rest of the staff. Discuss how and when they will be used.

We include sample performance indicator continua as illustrative examples in appendix C (page 153).

Assessment of Transdisciplinary Impacts

Most current assessments, both large scale and classroom based, target knowledge and skills in content areas. Such assessments are appropriate if the sole purpose of schooling is for students to learn the basics in traditional subjects. However, when our mission includes performance indicators taken from abstract transdisciplinary impacts—such as the 4Cs—then our assessment photo album must expand. In the whitepaper *Assessment of 21st Century Skills*, the Partnership for 21st Century Skills (2007) describes the need and the recommendations for future assessments:

> While the current assessment landscape is replete with assessments that measure knowledge of core content areas such as language arts, mathematics, science and social studies, there is a comparative lack of assessments and analyses focused on 21st century skills. Current tests fall short in several key ways:
>
> • The tests are not designed to gauge how well students apply what they know to new situations or evaluate how students might use technologies to solve problems or communicate ideas.
>
> • While teachers and schools are being asked to modify their practice based on standardized test data, the tests are not designed to help teachers make decisions about how to target their daily instruction.
>
> • Current testing systems are rarely designed to measure a school or district's contribution to learning from a student's first day until his or her last day. (pp. 1–2)

It proposes that needed assessments should "be largely performance-based and authentic, calling upon students to use 21st century skills" (Partnership for 21st Century Skills, 2007, p. 6). We heartily agree. One way to ensure assessments cover transdisciplinary impacts is to use the cornerstone tasks from our curriculum blueprint.

Cornerstone Tasks

As noted in chapter 4, we propose mapping a curriculum backward from long-term transfer impacts. The term *cornerstone* is meant to suggest that as a cornerstone anchors a building, these tasks should anchor the curriculum. Why? Because they engage learners in applying their learning as a means of providing evidence of their ability to transfer. In other words, they are manifestations of the impacts we seek—within and across subject areas.

Cornerstone tasks are performance tasks that elicit demonstrations of knowledge and skills valued in the wider world beyond school. The tasks may be content specific, covering mathematics, science, or social studies, or integrated, involving two or more content areas or mission-related outcomes.

Here are the general characteristics of cornerstone tasks; they:

- Are performance based, calling for the application and transfer of learning
- Establish authentic contexts for performance
- Recur across the grades, becoming increasingly sophisticated over time
- Integrate transdisciplinary impacts (such as critical thinking, technology use, and teamwork) with disciplinary content
- May be used as assessments or rich learning activities
- Include established indicators, rubrics, and performance continua for assessing student growth and achievement
- Engage students in relevant learning
- Are accompanied by analytic and developmental rubrics to enable longitudinal tracking of growth as well as learner self-assessment
- Provide evidence of achievement for student portfolios so that students graduate with a résumé of demonstrated accomplishments (impacts)

Cornerstone tasks are intended as *common* assessments; once identified, they are an expected part of the curriculum. While teachers may use different assessments in their units, all teachers will be expected to use these tasks with their students. Figure 5.5 shows the relationship among various types of assessments and the role of cornerstone tasks.

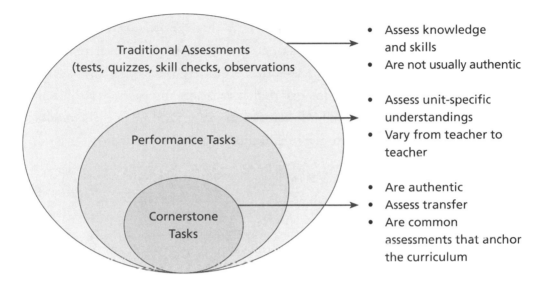

Figure 5.5: Cornerstone tasks and other types of assessments.

Figure 5.6 provides an example of a cornerstone task.

As a reporter for the Consumer Advisor website, your job is to investigate the pricing plans for three cell phone services in your area to determine the best value for different scenarios (a monthly plan, a two-year contract, a plan for a family of four, and so on). Include all potential costs in your analysis (price per call in minutes and price per text in megabytes; costs of a new phone; fees for early termination; and so on).

Your report will be posted online and should include:

- Your analysis of the three plans
- Tables, graphs, or equations to represent the costs for the various scenarios
- Your recommendations for consumers

Figure 5.6: Sample cornerstone task.

Such tasks encourage students to see meaningful learning as integrated rather than something that occurs in isolated subject silos.

Grafting

One natural way to integrate transdisciplinary impacts with existing academic tasks is through a process we call *grafting*. For example, let's say a disciplinary cornerstone task asks students to demonstrate their knowledge of ecosystem dynamics by investigating the effects of an introduction of an invasive species into a specific environment. Of course, they would need to apply all that they have learned about ecosystems to analyze this situation and propose a solution, but they would also need to call on their skills as systems thinkers. The teacher could select the following performance indicators as being appropriate to the task.

- The student identifies and explains how and why specific short- and long-term results may occur within an ecosystem due to the introduction of an invasive species.

- The student recognizes and describes how a system's organization influences its behaviors and changes over time.

- The student identifies elements of the system that are changing over time.

Teachers can apply this process to almost any rich performance task. Performance indicators for other transdisciplinary impacts could have been chosen, but we suggest being selective to ensure that the connections being made are authentic and not forced. In other words, effective application of the transdisciplinary impact should be essential to successful performance on the task.

Consider what happens when a teacher enhances a traditional and familiar task—a book report—by grafting the transdisciplinary impacts of *technology user*, *critical thinker*, and *communicator* onto it (figure 5.7).

Note that the original intent—a basic summary of the story—is addressed, but the task is enhanced through the addition of a technology application. Moreover, the use of technology, Bookhooks, opens up a real-world audience for authentic communication.

> **Traditional task:** Write a book report on *A Sick Day for Amos McGee* following the given format.
>
> **Grafted task:** You have been asked to submit a book review for *A Sick Day for Amos McGee* to post on the Bookhooks website. Thousands of kids visit this website to find out about books that they might like to read. Your review should summarize the basic plot, discuss the strengths and weaknesses of the writing, and make a recommendation. Before you begin, review other students' book reviews (www.bookhooks.com/browse.cfm) to see what makes an effective review.

Figure 5.7: Sample grafted assessment task.

The Literacy Design Collaborative (LDC) offers an excellent resource for constructing cornerstone tasks. The LDC has developed a series of generic task templates that teachers can customize. The task templates were originally created around the Common Core State Standards for English language arts (NGA & CCSSO, 2010a) in grades 6–12 with core content in science, social studies, and technical areas (Crawford, Galiatsos, & Lewis, 2011). The resulting cornerstone tasks call for students to read, analyze, and interpret text (both literary and informational) and then write cogent arguments, explanations, or narratives. We have found that the LDC templates lend themselves well to the design of performance tasks in general (not just for the CCSS) and are well suited to grafting with transdisciplinary impacts. Figure 5.8 (page 84) presents examples of two LDC templates with associated cornerstone tasks.

Notice in these examples that both tasks include the transdisciplinary impacts of *technology user*, *critical thinker*, and *communicator*. The second task also highlights a disposition.

It is not uncommon for teachers to say that transdisciplinary impacts have always been part of their performance tasks. They're probably right; they may have been there but often implicitly. We maintain that *if* transdisciplinary impacts are part of a school mission, *then* we need to assess them explicitly. In fact, we often miss relatively easy opportunities to make evidence of impact a common part of our assessment design practices. This grafting process can help us make use of what is already just below the surface.

Argumentation Task Template

After researching _____ (informational texts) on _____ (content topic or issue), write a/an _____ (essay or substitute) that argues your position on _____ (topic, issue, or essential question). Support your position with evidence from research. Be sure to cite your sources and acknowledge competing views. Give examples from past or current events issues to illustrate and clarify your position.

Task Example

After researching academic articles on the use of commercial drones (such as for package delivery), write a blog post that argues your position on whether commercial drones should be allowed and, if so, what regulations should be enacted. Support your position with evidence from your research. Be sure to cite your sources and acknowledge competing views.

Informational or Explanatory Task Template

Question: _____. After reading _____ (literature or informational texts), write a/an _____ (essay, report, article, or substitute) that defines and explains _____ (term or concept). Support your discussion with evidence from the texts. What _____ (conclusions or implications) can you draw?

Task Example

After reading stories about people who faced challenges and struggled to overcome them, write a cartoon story using an online tool (such as Stripgenerator) that defines and explains the importance of grit and determination when faced with a challenge. Your story should illustrate your conclusions about the value of determination and grit.

Source: Adapted from Literacy Design Collaborative, 2014.

Figure 5.8: Literacy Design Collaborative task templates and sample tasks.

Ideally, a curriculum planned backward from the long-term disciplinary and transdisciplinary impacts we seek is based on a series of cornerstone tasks that build over the years: the assessment side of the performance indicator continuum in figure 5.3 (page 76). These tasks would be recurring in nature, beginning in the younger grades as simple and highly scaffolded and progressing across the grades to become increasingly complex and authentic. Moreover, the learner's degree of autonomy would increase over time.

The selection and design of cornerstone tasks that recur across the grades is challenging work. Elementary teachers, in particular, may struggle to create developmentally appropriate tasks connected to long-term transfer goals since these are often seen as lofty and too difficult for younger learners. We have found it helpful to ask, "What task and associated product or performance could students at this grade level perform to demonstrate their growth toward this transfer goal?" In most cases, opportunities for students to demonstrate these transfer goals can usually be found at all levels, even early childhood. To ensure a coherent progression across the grades, we encourage the development of maps to organize and connect cornerstone tasks across grade levels and subject areas.

Cornerstone Task Maps

Cornerstone task maps specify performance indicators at particular stages of development. Figure 5.9 (page 86) presents a map of recurring cornerstone tasks developed at the International School of Beijing for a long-term transfer goal in science. The tasks were constructed around the identified performance areas that demonstrate developmentally appropriate performances for the transfer goal at the identified grade levels. Figure 5.8 also includes examples of grafting various transdisciplinary impacts onto these cornerstone tasks via performance indicators.

Cornerstone tasks for every transfer goal do not usually occur every year. Schools will develop their cornerstone maps to help spread these out across grade-levels and subject areas. For example, if science has three transfer goals (TG1, TG2, and TG3), cornerstone tasks for these may be distributed in the following way.

TG1: Prekindergarten, grade 2, grade 5, grade 8, and grade 11

TG2: Kindergarten, grade 3, grade 6, grade 9, and grade 12

TG3: Grade 1, grade 4, grade 7, and grade 10

This arrangement of cornerstone tasks also allows teachers to address learning needs revealed by these tasks over time. In other words, if a weakness surfaces in an area of TG1 in grade 2, it can be specifically addressed in grades 3 and 4 and re-assessed in grade 5. This arrangement links student growth in a longitudinal manner across similar performance areas and strands.

Figure 5.10 (page 89) presents a sample K–12 map of cornerstone tasks tied to long-term transfer goals for four main academic subjects. The tasks have been mapped backward from the identified long-term transfer goals within the disciplines, although you'll see that some of the tasks are transdisciplinary. You'll also note that the transdisciplinary impacts of the 4Cs have been grafted in various combinations onto these tasks.

Transfer Goal	Students will use scientific approaches and methodologies to investigate phenomena, claims, results, and information.				
Associated Skills	Asking Questions	Proposing Hypotheses	Devising Tests	Collecting Data	Drawing Conclusions

Recurring Cornerstone Tasks

Grade Level	Tasks	Transdisciplinary Impacts and Performance Indicators
Grade 9	Consumer Science Students will compare products by devising an appropriate line of scientific inquiry, carrying out research, and interpreting results. They will make a claim about the best product and communicate the inquiry, results, and interpretations of their findings. Others in the class will judge how well students communicate their claims most effectively. (Example: Design and conduct a controlled investigation to determine which diet or health care product has the best scientific backing for its claims and why people should purchase it.)	Communication • Clearly states claims and conclusions with convincing references to scientific evidence • Communicates data from sound investigations in a way that communicates claims and conclusions effectively • Uses and integrates a range of digital media (photography, audio, video, web production, digital editing, or presentation slides) to generate compelling and persuasive communication

continued →

Grade 7	Seek and Solve	Global Citizen
	Students will conduct research and test various potential solutions for sustainability issues in their simulated city by devising an appropriate line of scientific inquiry. They will assess the supporting data and claims for authenticity and make a recommendation based on these results. The students will communicate the inquiry, results, and interpretations of their findings. (Example: Propose a plan and procedure for collecting and recycling cooking oils from area restaurants and food carts to create more sustainable sources of energy.)	• Identifies elements of the system that are changing over time and require solutions to maintain sustainability • Explains how actions can create consequences, both wanted and unwanted • Evaluates the effectiveness and implications of existing solutions to issues
Grade 5	Prove It!	Communication
	Students devise and conduct a scientific test that is fair and free of bias. From this experience, students produce a procedure with the clarity and detail for others to replicate. After a peer conducts his or her test, results, and conclusions, students discuss them. (Example: Conduct controlled tests to see which brand of paper towel is most absorbent. Produce a "Prove It Guide" so that others can follow the procedure with clarity and accuracy.)	• Develops clear procedural guides • Uses appropriate tone and structure for the audience and purpose • Adds effectiveness to communications through the inclusion of graphics, data, digital elements, and so on

Source: International School of Beijing, 2013. Used with permission.

Figure 5.9: Sample map of recurring cornerstone tasks for science.

Recurring Cornerstone Tasks

Grade Level	Tasks	Transdisciplinary Impacts and Performance Indicators
Grade 2	**Create Your Own Experiment** Students follow the scientific method to answer one of their questions. Questioning, hypothesizing, experimenting, observing, and concluding are each broken down and examined individually. (Example: Observe and predict which objects a magnet will attract.)	Critical Thinking • Engages in discovery, exploration, and experimentation • Devises a question and develops a simple methodology to test possible answers • Uses observations to answer questions, construct a reasonable explanation, solve a problem, and create something
Early Years (PreK)	**Fair's Fair** Students are introduced to the concept of a fair test and use this to carry out a novel, simple investigation. They learn to ask questions that can be tested and attempt to create fair testing environments with adult support. Findings and conclusions are organized for communication. (Example: Will it float? Investigate the properties of various objects in terms of flotation in water. Develop simple hypotheses as to why some things float and others sink.)	Critical Thinking • Makes observations about the immediate environment • Makes simple judgments based on personal experience • Conducts basic tests and evaluations using simple criteria • Draws conclusions with references to personal observations

Grade	English Language Arts	Mathematics	Science	Social Studies
12	Independent Study Project ELA and Science or Social Studies [Critical Thinking, Communication]	Mathematical Modeling Project (Lifetime Savings and Investments) [Critical Thinking, Communication]	Independent Study Project ELA and Science or Social Studies [Critical Thinking, Communication]	Independent Study Project ELA and Science or Social Studies [Critical Thinking, Communication]
11	Parody or Satire Skit ELA and Science or Social Studies [Creativity, Collaboration, Communication]	Amusement Park Physics Linked to Science [Critical Thinking, Communication]	Chemistry Crime Scene [Critical Thinking, Collaboration, Communication]	Problem-Solution Campaign [Critical Thinking, Collaboration, Communication]
10	Original Short Story, Song, or Poem [Creativity, Communication]	How to Lie With Statistics Project [Critical Thinking, Collaboration, Communication]	Genetics Project Science and Social Studies [Critical Thinking, Communication]	Constitutional Checks and Balances [Critical Thinking, Communication]
9	Research Project With Audiovisual Presentation [Critical Thinking, Communication]	Mathematical Modeling With Linear Equations [Critical Thinking, Communication]	Earthquake Science [Critical Thinking, Collaboration, Communication]	Contemporary Issues Debate [Critical Thinking, Communication]

Figure 5.10: Sample K–12 map of cornerstone tasks tied to long-term transfer goals and the 4Cs.

continued →

Grade	English Language Arts	Mathematics	Science	Social Studies
8	Causes of Conflict Research Project ELA and Social Studies [Critical Thinking, Communication]	Design Your Dream Bedroom [Critical Thinking, Communication]	Consumer Scientist [Critical Thinking, Collaboration, Communication]	Causes of Conflict Research Project ELA and Social Studies [Critical Thinking, Communication]
7	Autobiography [Communication]	A Contractor's Proposal [Critical Thinking, Communication]	Water-Quality Testing [Critical Thinking, Communication]	History: Whose Story? Examining Perspectives [Critical Thinking]
6	Personal Narrative [Communication]	Exercise Studies Science and Health or Physical Education [Critical Thinking, Creativity, Collaboration]	Prove It! [Critical Thinking, Communication]	Humans and the Environment [Critical Thinking, Communication]
5	People on the Move Research Project ELA and Social Studies [Critical Thinking, Communication]	Fund-Raiser Project [Critical Thinking, Creativity, Collaboration, Communication]	Conduct Your Own Experiment [Critical Thinking, Communication]	People on the Move Research Project ELA and Social Studies [Critical Thinking, Communication]

4	Authors' Party Presentations [Collaboration, Communication]	Geometry Town [Critical Thinking, Creativity, Collaboration]	Seed to Plant Project [Critical Thinking, Collaboration, Communication]	Where We Live and How We Live [Critical Thinking, Communication]
3	Personal Narrative [Creativity, Communication]	Measure This! [Critical Thinking, Creativity, Collaboration]	Prove It! [Critical Thinking, Communication]	Alike and Different [Critical Thinking, Collaboration]
2	How-To Booklet and Presentation [Communication]	Animal Zoo (Habitats) STEM Project [Critical Thinking, Creativity, Collaboration]	Animal Zoo (Habitats) STEM Project [Critical Thinking, Creativity, Collaboration]	Wants and Needs [Critical Thinking, Communication]
1	Kinder Kid Advice [Creativity, Communication]	Party Time [Creativity, Collaboration]	Will It Float? [Critical Thinking, Collaboration]	Me and My Family [Creativity, Communication]
K	Letter Songs [Creativity]	Number Maze [Creativity, Collaboration, Communication]	Observing Carefully With All Senses [Critical Thinking]	All About Me [Creativity, Communication]

The examples in this figure suggest a somewhat standardized assessment system in that they are designed as part of the curriculum and intended for all students. However, districts and schools may elect to allow some choice for teachers and students in this system. For example, a teacher may use a different task as long as it will provide appropriate evidence of the targeted transfer goals and strands. A more personalized approach for students would enable them to propose a task or project through which they could provide evidence of performance against one or more of the targeted transfer goals.

Rubrics

We noted earlier that a characteristic of strong cornerstone tasks is that they can be assessed using established criteria. A rubric is an evaluation tool combining established criteria with a performance scale. Rubrics judge students' responses to open-ended assignments, performance tasks, and projects. Well-developed rubrics have several virtues.

- They specify the salient criteria for judging student performance.
- They help clarify instructional goals and serve as targets for teaching and learning.
- They provide specific feedback to learners and teachers.
- They guide students in self-assessment.

Moreover, when grade-level or department teams of teachers use common rubrics, we see improved reliability, such as more consistent evaluation of student performance (Goldberg & Roswell, 1998).

There are many sources of well-developed rubrics for evaluating student products and performances within academic subject areas. However, when assessing broader transdisciplinary impacts, educators may have to construct their own. Identifying a list of performance indicators is an important first step. These can then be incorporated into an analytic rubric or developmental continuum. Figure 5.11 provides an example for the skill of collaboration, one of the 4Cs.

Performance Indicators for Collaboration	Works Toward the Achievement of Group Goals	Demonstrates Effective Interpersonal Skills	Contributes to Group Maintenance	Effectively Performs a Variety of Roles Within a Group
4—Expert	Actively helps identify group goals and works hard to meet them	Actively promotes effective group interaction and the expression of ideas and opinions in a way that is sensitive to the feelings and knowledge base of others	Actively helps the group identify changes or modifications necessary in the group process and works toward carrying out those changes	Expertly performs multiple roles within the group
3—Practitioner	Communicates commitment to the group goals and effectively carries out assigned roles	Participates in group interaction without prompting and expresses ideas and opinions in a way that is sensitive to the feelings and knowledge base of others	Helps identify changes or modifications necessary in the group process and works toward carrying out those changes	Adequately performs more than a single role within the group
2—Apprentice	Communicates a commitment to the group goals but does not carry out assigned roles	Participates in group interaction with prompting or expresses ideas and opinions without considering the feelings and knowledge base of others	When prompted, helps identify changes or modifications necessary in the group process or is only minimally involved in carrying out those changes	Makes an attempt to perform more than one role within the group but has little success with secondary roles
1—Novice	Does not work toward group goals or actively works against them	Does not participate in group interaction, even with prompting, or expresses ideas and opinions in a way that is insensitive to the feelings and knowledge base of others	Does not attempt to identify changes or modifications necessary in the group process, even when prompted, or refuses to work toward carrying out those changes	Does not attempt to perform a designated role, even when prompted, or refuses to play a supportive role

Source: Adapted from Marzano, Pickering, & McTighe, 1993.

Figure 5.11: Sample analytic rubric for collaboration.

For more examples of rubrics for transdisciplinary impacts, see the following websites (visit **go.solution-tree.com/leadership** to access live links).

- EdLeader21 (www.edleader21.com/order.php)
- Catalina Foothills School District's Global Citizen Lifelong Learners (www.cfsd16.org/public/_century/pdf/Rubrics /CFSDCritical&CreativeThinkingRubrics.pdf)
- DoDEA21 (https://content.dodea.edu/VS/21st_century/web/21/21 _skills_reflection_evaluation_rubrics.html)

While we believe that rubrics for cornerstone tasks offer rich assessment evidence of understanding, transfer, and mission-related outcomes, there is certainly a role for more traditional assessments in rounding out the photo album. Of course, teachers will continue to employ tests and quizzes to check on acquisition of knowledge and skills. External, standardized assessments, including state or provincial tests, Advanced Placement tests, and International Baccalaureate exams, offer measures of achievement that allow for comparisons across schools, districts, states, and even nations.

Other forms of assessment will likely be needed to appraise some of the more elusive traits and skills contained in mission statements. For example, some schools use learning-style diagnostic tools with their students. Gallup's StrengthsFinder 2.0 is a popular program in the corporate world but can also be helpful in profiling students' aptitudes. Similarly, the grit survey from the University of Pennsylvania purports to measure one's resilience and perseverance.

We also recommend that students regularly self-assess any of the soft skills and dispositions included in your mission. Such assessments can contribute to a growing pool of student data.

Conclusion

In this chapter, we explored the elements of a comprehensive system for assessing *all* of our goals—including the broader goals contained in our mission—not just the ones that are easiest to test and grade. Now we can say that an intentional curriculum and assessment framework fully supports the enactment of our vision, and we can use the resulting student performance data to check that we are on track toward the 21st century learning we seek.

In the next chapter, we move to stage 3 of backward design to consider the kind of instruction needed to achieve our mission. We will also describe the value of identifying an explicit set of learning principles to guide the selection of teaching strategies and resources for 21st century learning and introduce a framework for aligning teaching methods with our various goals.

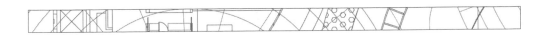

CHAPTER 6

Instruction for Modern Learning

How do we align instructional practices, resources, and tools with our goals for modern learning?

What kind of teaching and learning would you expect to see in a school or district committed to the kinds of impacts described in this book? Would we see kids seated in rows diligently taking notes based on a teacher's lecture? Would we see students working in groups on a collaborative project? Might we see students with headphones working individually at computer stations to complete competency-based learning modules? Or students learning in a virtual space outside of a traditional school building? These and any number of variations are possible. But how should we determine the future of teaching and learning?

So far, we have defined our ideal future, created a vision and mission reflective of that future, and identified desired impacts. Using a backward design process, we've developed a curriculum blueprint around these impacts so we know where we're going, and we've considered the cornerstone tasks and other assessment evidence that will provide measures of success. Now that we know exactly what we're assessing and how we're assessing it, we can step back and flesh out the learning plan needed to help us get there.

In this chapter, we will consider approaches to instruction suited to 21st century learning. We'll begin with a discussion of the value of having an explicit set of learning principles for your school to guide teaching and professional development. We will then examine the Acquisition, Meaning Making, Transfer framework and its implications for instructional practice. Finally, we'll explore ideas for personalizing learning and showcase examples of strategic tools to support learners in the development of targeted impacts.

Learning Principles

Before we discuss various approaches to learning and specific teaching methods, we recommend a more general consideration of learning principles. Indeed, the confluence of research from cognitive psychology (Bransford, Brown, & Cocking, 2000; Hattie, 2009), studies of student achievement (Newmann, Bryk, & Nagaoka, 2001), and neuroscience (Willis, 2006) provides educators with a robust compass to chart the course of modern learning. A practical way for schools to operationalize this knowledge base is to identify learning principles that reflect research and best practice to guide instruction.

For example, in their article "An Implementation Framework to Support 21st Century Skills," Jay McTighe and Elliott Seif (2010) present the following set of learning principles. Notice that this format features a principle of learning followed by specific implications for classroom practice.

1. Learning is purposeful and contextual. *Therefore, students should be helped to see the purpose in what they are asked to learn. Learning should be framed by relevant questions, meaningful challenges, and authentic applications.*

2. Experts organize or chunk their knowledge around transferable, core concepts ("big ideas") that guide their thinking about the domain and help them integrate new knowledge. *Therefore, content instruction should be framed in terms of core ideas and transferable processes, not as discrete facts and skills.*

3. Different types of thinking, such as classification and categorization, inferential reasoning, analysis, synthesis, and metacognition, mediate and enhance learning. *Therefore, learning events should engage students in "higher order thinking" to deepen and apply their learning.*

4. Learners reveal and demonstrate their understanding when they can apply, transfer, and adapt their learning to new and novel situations and problems. *Therefore, teachers should teach for transfer, and students should have multiple opportunities to apply their learning in meaningful and varied contexts.*

5. New learning is built on prior knowledge. Learners use their experiences and background knowledge to actively construct meaning about themselves and the world around them. *Therefore, students must be helped to actively connect new information and ideas to what they already know.*

6. Learning is social. *Therefore, teachers should provide opportunities for interactive learning in a supportive environment.*

7. Attitudes and values mediate learning by filtering experiences and perceptions. *Therefore, teachers should help students make their attitudes and values explicit and understand how they influence learning.*

8. Learning is nonlinear; it develops and deepens over time. *Therefore, students should be involved in revisiting core ideas and processes so as to develop deeper and more sophisticated learning over time.*

9. Models of excellence and ongoing feedback enhance learning and performance. *Therefore, learners need to see models of excellent work and be provided with regular, timely, and user-friendly feedback in order to practice, retry, rethink, and revise their work.*

10. Effectively accommodating a learner's preferred learning style, prior knowledge, and interests enhances learning. *Therefore, teachers should pre-assess to find out students' prior knowledge, learning preference, and interests. They should differentiate their instruction to address the significant differences they discover.* (p. 153)

One approach to identifying learning principles is to charge a small committee with the job of conducting a review of research on learning and examining previously developed compilations of principles (see Brandt, 1998; Wiggins & McTighe, 2007) in order to recommend a set to the larger staff. However, most busy educators we know would find it difficult to devote time to such an activity, given the myriad other duties they perform.

A more efficient approach to identifying learning principles is realized through an exercise known as Best Learning that Jay and his colleague Grant Wiggins have used for years. This inductive exercise is designed to engage educators in reflecting on their own experiences of deep and meaningful learning and then extracting the characteristics of those experiences. Through this process, school staff or grade-level or department teams can identify a set of learning principles to guide their actions.

The Best Learning Exercise

This exercise has three parts. First, ask participants to think of a specific experience in their life in which their learning was profound. We encourage people not to limit their thinking to traditional schooling. In fact, many of the examples people identify come from outside of school, such as learning a new hobby. Then have them list the characteristics of that learning experience. In other words, what were the elements that were most impactful on their learning (for instance, the goals, sequence, resources, methods, assessments, and so on)? Allow three to four minutes for individual thinking and writing.

Second, have participants share their personal lists within groups of four or five people, and listen for common elements from the diverse examples shared. A recorder should make a list of the generalizations from the group sharing. Allow eight to twelve minutes for sharing and generalizing, depending on group size.

Finally, ask each group to share *one* of the common characteristics that group members identified, and publicly post these with a projector or on chart paper. Rotate from group to group until all common ideas are posted as a master list. This takes approximately eight to twelve minutes.

The similarity in responses among diverse groups from all over the world is striking. Following is a representative list of characteristics of deep learning experiences derived from this exercise. Learning is deep and meaningful when:

- Learners know the learning goals and how they will be assessed (there is no mystery or uncertainty about the end result)
- Learners see the goals as relevant and worthwhile

- Learning and assessment tasks are authentic (emphasis on relevant, real-world applications)

- The evaluative criteria, such as rubrics, are presented and explained at the beginning

- Models of excellence are shared to provide a clear picture of desired quality

- Ongoing assessments provide detailed feedback for the learners

- Learners have opportunities to practice, refine, or redo their work after feedback is given

- Learners understand that it is OK to make mistakes when learning something new

- There is often the opportunity to collaborate with others

- Learners have some choice in terms of how they show what they have learned via products and performances

- The teacher or instructor functions like a coach or an advocate rather than as an adversary

- Learners are encouraged to reflect on their learning and set future goals based on the assessment results

In order to build understanding and ownership, we strongly recommend that school staff be actively involved in the process of identifying shared principles of learning. Figure 6.1 (page 102) presents one process for doing this.

Once the district, school, or department identifies the learning principles, it has a common language for conversations about teaching and learning to actively use. The principles function as criteria for a variety of school actions, including choosing among various instructional strategies, selecting resources such as textbooks and software, and identifying look-for indicators during classroom observations. Note that any set of learning principles that a school adopts should not be set in stone. Staff can (and should) periodically revisit and refine these principles to reflect emerging research and insights.

Goal: An agreed-on set of learning principles for a school or department

Protocol

Step 1: Discuss the goal and intent of agreeing on a common set of learning principles.

Step 2: Engage staff in the Best Learning exercise. Collect and compile a draft of responses. (Note: Parents and students could also be involved in this exercise.)

Step 3: Circulate the draft list of responses to the Best Learning exercise to staff groups, such as grade-level teams, departments, division levels, and so on, for their review and recommendations. Questions for group consideration include the following.

- Does the list reflect all the important learning principles?

- Are the principles clearly stated and understandable?

- What does each principle imply for our work? Would some established practices need to be changed to better align with a stated principle?

(Note: Additional examples of developed learning principles can also be reviewed at this time.)

Step 4: Each group submits suggested edits, additions, and deletions to a desig-nated team, which reviews the recommendations of the various groups and com-piles a synthesized and edited list.

Step 5: The edited list of learning principles circulates for a second review. If the group proposes major edits, the process continues until a generally agreed-on set of learning principles is produced.

Step 6 (optional, but encouraged): The final list of learning principles is presented for staff review and sign-off. By signing, staff members commit to accepting and agreeing to act on the agreed-on learning principles.

Figure 6.1: A protocol for identifying learning principles.

*Visit **go.solution-tree.com/leadership** for a reproducible version of this figure.*

Backward Design of Instruction at the Classroom Level

It's important to remember that whether building a districtwide curriculum or planning classroom instruction, you should avoid jumping to stage 3 of the backward design process before you have clarity about the desired results you seek (stage 1) and the evidence of success for learning (stage 2). Too often, we find teachers' planning focuses on what their students "will do on Monday" in terms of activities to do, texts to read, or content to cover. Of course, we need to plan and sequence our day-to-day actions, but we also need to recognize that teaching is a means to an end. Our instructional methods, students' learning experiences, and the resources we employ should all be directed toward the end goals, and different goals call for different methods.

The Acquisition, Meaning Making, Transfer (AMT) framework covers three interrelated yet distinct goals that have concomitant implications for the teacher's *and* the learner's roles and actions.

Acquisition

Acquisition refers to the goal of learning basic information and skills. Generally speaking, the goal of acquisition is automaticity; we want students to be able to recall facts on demand, like times tables or verb conjugations in another language, and to perform basic skills without thinking, like dribbling a basketball or shifting gears. Arguably, traditional education was largely an acquisition-based enterprise, whereby students committed finite bodies of knowledge to memory via rote learning. While certain basics, such as learning to read, will no doubt remain fundamental education goals, the power of technology to enable immediate access to knowledge raises important questions for schooling. For example, what information should one commit to memory versus be able to access? What basic skills may become obsolete, given widely available apps (consider spelling, addition, and map reading)?

The role of the teacher here is to help learners acquire targeted knowledge and skills using tried-and-true teaching methods, including direct presentation, lecture, questioning, and modeling or skill practicing.

The learner's role is to acquire information. Learners must listen attentively and take notes, read and view carefully, apply mnemonic techniques, and rehearse. To develop proficiency in a skill, learners should carefully watch an expert demonstrate the skill, diligently practice the skill, and seek and use feedback to improve their performance.

Meaning Making

Understanding is qualitatively different than knowing something. Haven't we all seen students who know historical facts without understanding their import? How about the learner who can memorize a mathematical algorithm and plug in numbers on a worksheet but doesn't understand *when* to use the algorithm in a more complex problem situation? Someone who really understands something can explain it effectively in his or her own words, can make new connections to it, can apply it to new contexts, and can see it from different points of view.

It is our contention that such understanding *must be earned* through deliberate intellectual effort. While one can acquire factual knowledge through rote learning and memorization and develop proficiency in a basic skill through diligent practice, the goal of understanding requires the active process of meaning making. (Think about the aha experience when one understands a joke.) Indeed, the phrase *come to an understanding* signals that it is unlikely that a learner will fully grasp an abstract idea just by reading or hearing it. Instead, he or she must think about it, try to connect it to something familiar, question it, try it out, look at it from a different point of view, make and test inferences about it, and reconsider it.

Since the understanding of abstract ideas must be ultimately constructed in the learner's mind, a teacher cannot simply transmit insight by telling. We think a significant role shift is required, whereby the instructor moves from a disseminator of knowledge to a *facilitator of meaning making*. Operationally, this means that the teacher needs to become more of a Socratic questioner, a problem poser, and a devil's advocate in order to help learners grasp the meaning of important concepts and processes. To help students arrive at understandings, the teacher will also need to design different activities than those they may use to further acquisition of knowledge and skills.

The learner's role is to be active. One cannot simply sit back passively and develop deep understanding. The learner must engage by considering and reconsidering an idea, examining different points of view, trying varied solution pathways, raising questions, and applying his or her understanding in new contexts.

Transfer

Closely related to understanding, *transfer*—as noted previously in relation to goals—refers to the process of effectively applying one's learning in a situation different than it was learned in. For example, a student may know multiplication, but does she understand how and when it applies in a particular situation?

Transfer calls for thoughtful application; after all, one must adapt to different circumstances, audiences, and constraints when using knowledge in authentic situations.

Coaches in athletics and the arts offer a good example of a teacher's role when helping students develop the capacity to transfer learning. Coaches model desired performances and then offer corrective feedback as the learner tries to apply his or her learning. They understand that the learner needs many opportunities to try to perform in increasingly novel and complex situations in order to develop transfer capabilities.

Interestingly, the ultimate goal of transfer is to make the teacher or coach barely needed. Therefore, over time, a teacher should gradually remove support and scaffolding so that students learn to transfer learning on their own. Of course, there is a role for direct instruction and modeling, but always in the context of trying to improve (increasingly autonomous) transfer performance on worthy tasks.

Table 6.1 (page 106) provides a summary of general teaching approaches related to the goals of the AMT framework.

We do not suggest that the categories are pure or rigid. Indeed, many of the meaning-making strategies, such as comparing and creating graphic representations or organizers, also help learners remember factual information, thus tying into acquisition. Nonetheless, we think that the general intentions and methods are qualitatively different and will prove useful to teachers and students.

Backward Design of the Learning Plan

The same tendency some teachers have to plan daily activities and jump from stage 1 to stage 3 can also happen at the school and district levels in the inclination to adopt and implement various educational approaches (such as project-based learning) and developed programs (such as a new mathematics textbook series or an International Baccalaureate program). Indeed, many strategic plans are full of well-intentioned commitments to "do" project-based learning, increase the use of technology, or implement character programs and the like with little, if any, evidence that these approaches are proven to be the best ways to achieve the impacts we seek. While any and all of these approaches and programs *may* have value, their selection should be the result of a because-then analysis—*because* our mission calls for X impact, *then* we have chosen Y input as a means to achieve it. In other words,

Table 6.1: Learning Goals and Instructional Practices

Acquisition	Meaning Making	Transfer
This goal seeks to help learners acquire factual information and basic skills.	This goal seeks to help students construct meaning (come to an understanding) of important ideas and processes.	This goal seeks to support the learner's ability to transfer his or her learning autonomously and effectively in new situations.
Teacher Role: Direct Instruction In this role, the teacher informs the learners through explicit instruction in targeted knowledge and skills, differentiating as needed. Strategies include: • Diagnostic assessment • Lecture • Advanced organizers • Graphic organizers • Questioning • Demonstration • Modeling of approach • Process guides • Guided practice • Feedback and corrections • Differentiation	Teacher Role: Facilitative Teaching Teachers in this role engage the learners in actively processing information and guide their inquiry into complex problems, texts, projects, cases, or simulations—differentiating as needed. Strategies include: • Diagnostic assessment • Analogies • Comparison • Graphic representations or organizers • Divergent questions and probes • Concept attainment • Inquiry approaches • Problem-based learning • Socratic seminar • Reciprocal teaching • Formative (ongoing) assessments • Understanding notebooks • Feedback and corrections • Rethinking and reflection prompts	Teacher Role: Coaching In a coaching role, teachers establish clear performance goals, supervise ongoing opportunities to perform (independent practice) in increasingly complex situations, provide models, and give ongoing feedback (as personalized as possible). They also provide just-in-time teaching (direct support) when needed. Strategies include: • Ongoing assessment • Specific feedback in the context of authentic application • Conferences • Self-assessment and reflection prompts

Source: Adapted from Wiggins & McTighe, 2011.

backward design applies to the choice of all instructional approaches and learning resources—from the textbooks to the software to the developed programs—at the system level, not just the teacher level. Before beginning down a specific path, we need to seek evidence that an adopted instructional approach or program would help us achieve the impacts we desire based on evidence of student learning and performance.

Our recommendation here is straightforward: do not rush to select instructional approaches or programs until you have followed the design steps discussed up to this point. Indeed, our inclusion of the Input-Output-Impact and backward design frameworks is to remind you to avoid action planning and implementation before your goals are crystal clear and you know what measures of success will look like. We urge schools and districts, as well as teachers, to connect instructional approaches or program selections directly with desired impacts and continuously look for evidence as to whether these are contributing to the meeting of those impacts.

The AMT framework becomes even more powerful in a technological world that focuses on transdisciplinary impacts at both the classroom level and the school or district level. The framework's goals associated with learning academic content and processes converge with 21st century skills on several important points. Namely, transdisciplinary education should cultivate productive habits of mind or dispositions, connect technology and learning, and personalize learning—all while keeping the end goal in mind.

Cultivating Habits of Mind

As noted in chapter 5, Costa and Kallick (2008) identify sixteen habits of mind that, arguably, are critical for effective thinkers and self-directed learners—in school, in the workplace, and throughout life. We'll take a closer look at them here.

The habits of mind are problem-solving life skills students need to effectively operate in society. They promote strategic reasoning, insightfulness, perseverance, creativity, and craftsmanship. The understanding and application of these sixteen habits of mind serve to provide the individual with skills to work through real-life situations and respond using awareness, thought, and intentional strategy to gain a positive outcome (Costa & Kallick, 2000, 2008).

1. **Persisting:** Stick to the task at hand, follow through to completion, and remain focused.

2. **Managing impulsivity:** Take time to consider options, think before speaking or acting, remain calm when stressed or challenged, be thoughtful and considerate of others, and proceed carefully.

3. **Listening with understanding and empathy:** Pay attention to and do not dismiss another person's thoughts, feelings, and ideas; seek to put yourself in the other person's shoes; tell others when you can relate to what they are expressing; and hold thoughts at a distance in order to respect another person's point of view and feelings.

4. **Thinking flexibly:** Be able to change perspective, consider the input of others, generate alternatives, and weigh options.

5. **Thinking about thinking (metacognition):** Be aware of your thoughts, feelings, intentions, and actions; know that what you do and say affects others; and be willing to consider the impact of choices on yourself and others.

6. **Striving for accuracy:** Check for errors, measure at least twice, and nurture a desire for exactness, fidelity, and craftsmanship.

7. **Questioning and posing problems:** Ask yourself, "How do I know?"; develop a questioning attitude; consider what information is needed, and choose strategies to get that information; and consider the obstacles that need to be resolved.

8. **Applying past knowledge to new situations:** Use what is learned, consider prior knowledge and experience, and apply knowledge beyond the situation in which it was learned.

9. **Thinking and communicating with clarity and precision:** Strive to be clear and accurate when speaking and writing, and avoid generalizations, distortions, minimizations, and deletions when speaking and writing.

10. **Gathering data through all senses:** Stop to observe what you see, listen to what you hear, take note of what you smell, taste what you are eating, and feel what you are touching.

11. **Creating, imagining, and innovating:** Think about how something might be done differently from the norm, propose new ideas, strive for originality, and consider novel suggestions others might make.

12. **Responding with wonderment and awe:** Let the world's beauty, nature's power, and the vastness of the universe intrigue you; have regard for what is awe inspiring and can touch your heart; and be open to the little and big surprises in life you see in others and yourself.

13. **Taking responsible risks:** Be willing to try something new and different, consider doing things that are safe and sane even though they are new, and face your fear of making mistakes or of coming up short while refusing to let it stop you.

14. **Finding humor:** Be willing to laugh appropriately; look for the whimsical, absurd, ironic, and unexpected in life; and laugh at yourself when you can.

15. **Thinking interdependently:** Be willing to work with others and welcome their input and perspective, abide by decisions the work group makes even if you disagree somewhat, and be willing to learn from others in reciprocal situations.

16. **Remaining open to continuous learning:** Stay open to new experiences to learn from, be proud and humble enough to admit when you don't know, and welcome new information on all subjects.

These habits of mind can be highlighted throughout a curriculum, across the grades, and inside and outside of school. In fact, we anticipate that these elements will be closely linked with the transdisciplinary impacts you defined earlier. We propose that these habits be introduced *explicitly* when they are appropriate and necessary for performance on the cornerstone tasks described in chapter 5. Here is a sample seven-step process for doing this.

1. Introduce a specific disposition when it is necessary for success on a particular task or assignment.

2. Provide a variety of examples of people demonstrating the disposition inside and outside of school, as well as from literature, history, science, the arts, and so on.

3. Develop (ideally with the students) a list of developmentally appropriate, observable performance indicators for this disposition; for instance, what would we see and hear in a person who is *striving for accuracy*?

4. Remind students why this disposition is important and how they should use it within and beyond the school.

5. Using the list of observable performance indicators, give specific feedback to students relative to their demonstration of the disposition. Peer feedback can also be provided.

6. Have students self-assess their use of the disposition on the task. Ask them to identify other places and times when this disposition can be fruitfully enacted.

7. Encourage learners to set goals around improving specific habits of mind.

By highlighting dispositions overtly, educators signal to students that these habits are valued and valuable—in school, on the job, and throughout their lives. They are essential for success and part of achieving your impacts.

Connecting Technology and Learning

No discussion of 21st century schooling can exclude technology as an increasingly influential factor in teaching and learning. In fact, the confluence of two noteworthy trends—(1) ever-expanding sources of information and learning and (2) increasing availability of technologies for accessing this information—promise to be an educational game changer. Consider the following statistics presented in the infographic "What Is the Future of Education" (e-Learning Industry, 2014).

• Fifty percent of all Americans own either a tablet or an ebook reader.

• Seventy-nine percent of U.S. households have a computer.

• Seventy-five percent of U.S. households have Internet access at home.

• Fifty-eight percent of Americans own a smartphone.

• Three times as many students entering college had a tablet in 2012 than in 2011.

- Ninety percent of college students and high school seniors see tablets as valuable educational tools.

- Sixty-three percent of college students and high school seniors believe tablets will transform the way college students learn in the future.

- Six out of ten college students prefer digital formats when reading books inside or outside of class.

Predictably, these numbers will continue to expand and shape the nature of education within and beyond traditional classrooms and schools.

While we agree that technology offers new educational opportunities, we have often seen the use of educational technology portrayed as synonymous with 21st century learning. This pairing conflates ends and means. It's certainly not that we don't believe that technology is a major driver of change in education, but, like any approach, technology needs to be utilized in conjunction with a tight alignment to desired impacts. It's not a matter of "doing more technology"; it's a matter of making use of appropriate technologies in ways that enhance the achievement of desired results. In fact, grouping technological tools and processes in terms of their support for specific and varied learning outcomes and impacts is a useful way to help keep the focus on the achievement of these goals, not simply on the use of a given technological tool. (See McTighe & March, 2015.)

One such example can be seen in the movement toward flipped classrooms, whereby students watch online video tutorials outside of traditional class time to get the content typically presented through teacher lectures. Teachers can then devote class time to more active learning experiences that call for the application of knowledge. (See Miller, 2012.) In and of itself, such a practice does not constitute 21st century learning as much as it simply offers another delivery system for learning traditional subject matter. Indeed, much of the content available online is canned and standardized. However, a flipped instructional approach can free face-to-face classroom time for more impactful learning experiences beyond the transmission of content (for instance, greater emphasis on problem solving, discussion and debate, the development of 21st century skills, and hands-on applications).

For us, the key question is not, Should we move to flipped classrooms? Rather, it is, In what ways can a flipped-classroom approach enable us to better realize our targeted impacts? In fact, the first question should be, If too much of our face-to-face time is consumed with acquisition, and we don't have enough time to effectively approach impacts, how do we shift the way in which we use the time we have? In this case, a flipped approach is the answer to a dilemma, not simply an approach we have chosen. When using backward design, *if* we decide that flipped learning can help us deal with this dilemma, *then* the question becomes, Now that we have liberated part of class time from the acquisition of basic content knowledge and skills acquisition, what is the best use of face-to-face time with students for realizing our priority impacts?

The widening access to increasingly affordable information technologies, combined with the expansion of online learning resources, changes the education landscape. No longer will teachers in brick-and-mortar schoolrooms be the sole wellspring of wisdom. The potential exists for learners to access the world's knowledge on a 24-7 basis, and they can tailor their learning to their interests and needs. There are many free or low-cost sources for anytime-anywhere access to learning resources. Here are three examples.

1. **Khan Academy:** Khan Academy (www.khanacademy.org) offers an enormous online library of free content to enable people to learn about anything. Users have 24-7 access to thousands of topics in mathematics, science, and the humanities on any computer, tablet, or smartphone connected to the Internet. In fact, the emergence of Khan Academy helped popularize the concept of a flipped classroom.

2. **edX:** An online learning collaborative, edX (www.edx.org) is a partnership between Harvard University and MIT. Online classes are free and available to anyone in the world, covering such subjects as computer science, calculus, geometry, algebra, English, physics, biology, chemistry, Spanish, French, history, statistics, and psychology. Initially, the project developed course materials for higher education but has begun offering courses geared toward high school students.

3. **The Online Schools for Boys and for Girls:** These programs (www .onlineschoolforboys.org; www.onlineschoolforgirls.org) offer a platform for connecting learners throughout the world through

relevant and engaging coursework in a dynamic online learning community.

A crucial understanding regarding technology and 21st century learning has to do with the effect technology has had on changing the *context* for thinking about transdisciplinary outcomes. For example, consider the skill of collaboration. While the need to work effectively with others is certainly not a new outcome, the context for collaborating in the 21st century has changed dramatically. Synchronous and asynchronous collaboration platforms, along with the ability to chunk and distribute parts of larger tasks around the globe via shared project spaces, have changed the nature of collaboration. While the general definition of *collaboration* remains timeless, the skills and approaches needed to be a successful collaborator have shifted and will continue to shift. The same could be said of the other Cs—communication in a multimodal digital age, critical thinking in a time of seemingly boundless information, or creativity in an era where access to innovative tools is open and amplifies our creative capacities. In sum, think of technology not as an end but as an approach to 21st century learning that can enhance our capacity to help learners achieve targeted impacts.

Personalizing Learning

Personalized learning is a term with varying meanings. Previously, we discussed the importance of creating an operational definition for such terms to make sure everyone stays on the same page. To us, personalized learning is evident when:

- Students have some opportunities to explore topics of their choosing rather than following a totally prescribed curriculum

- Students can learn through a variety of means and sources in a more self-directed way

- Students can access knowledge through a 24-7, anywhere-anytime approach, not just from a teacher in a classroom

- Students have some choice in the ways in which they will demonstrate the desired goals of learning, including disciplinary and transdisciplinary impacts

- Teachers work as coaches to cocreate learning outcomes, experiences, and products with their students

- Schedules are flexible to meet the specific learning goals and processes of individual students, as opposed to bending learning to meet a fixed schedule

- Reports of learning are personalized rather than standardized; for instance, grades are based solely on grade-level standards

Table 6.2 presents a general planning framework of options for personalizing learning. The previous list of characteristics, along with these options, suggests that personalized learning is less of an instructional approach than it is a set of beliefs about learning (that allowing student input enhances motivation and effort), a set of appropriate choices for learners, and an environment that supports them.

Personalized learning can serve as an excellent vehicle to address both disciplinary and transdisciplinary impacts. In the case of disciplinary impacts, a personalized learning environment encourages independence and the demonstration of transfer goals within novel contexts. Personalized learning supports the development of transdisciplinary impacts in two powerful and mutually supportive ways. First, the skills associated with transdisciplinary impacts, such as the 4Cs, support the attainment of academic outcomes and disciplinary impacts. Since these impacts and related skills are essential to success, they are seen as valuable in school, much as they are in the wider world. Second, a personalized learning environment can, by its very nature, provide a rich and authentic context within which students can purposefully learn and apply skills, tools, and strategies on a regular basis. Thus, transdisciplinary impacts can be viewed as both means and ends!

In addition, as stated in the book *Learning Personalized: The Evolution of the Contemporary Classroom* (Zmuda, Curtis, & Ullman, 2015), personalized learning is an approach well suited to developing both disciplinary and transdisciplinary impacts (called *disciplinary outcomes* and *cross-disciplinary outcomes* in this book): "Personalized learning is a means to achieve those ends: a way to grow our children so they are better equipped to handle the uncertainty, complexity and excitement of the world" (pp. 23–24).

Table 6.2: A Personalized Learning Framework

Content	Process	Product	Reporting
Students have some choice regarding: • The topics they explore within an established curriculum • The topics or skills they pursue beyond the established curriculum content in support of stated goals • The resources that support their learning (such as textbook versus online sources)	Students have some choice regarding: • The learning activities (such as the selection of learning stations) • How they work (such as individually or in a team) • When and where they work (such as in class, at home, outside of school, or online) • How long the time frame for learning is	Students have some choice regarding: • The products and performances they develop to support their learning • The role, audience, and context for authentic tasks • The evidence they provide to document their learning based on stated goals	Reports on student achievement: • Profile individual performance and achievement on both disciplinary and transdisciplinary impacts (versus norm-referenced grading and reporting) • Highlight growth and progress for individuals • Separate work habits from achievement

Cognitive Tools for Today's Learners

As 21st century education evolves, the cultivation of independent, self-directed learners takes on greater import. One effective way to support student growth and development is through the use of cognitive tools. Jay McTighe and Frank Lyman (1988) describe cognitive tools as manifestations of sound theory and practice embedded in a concrete form. They serve to make the abstract processes of thinking and learning tangible and render the invisible visible.

The notion of using cognitive tools as part of an instructional approach requires, again, a shift in thinking about what the *teacher will do* to focus on what the *students will need* in order to achieve desired impacts. Indeed, the ultimate goal of transfer is for the learner to be able to apply his or her learning to new, authentic situations and to do this increasingly on his or her own without excessive teacher direction or scaffolding.

We propose two general types of cognitive tools to support learning for both disciplinary and transdisciplinary impacts: (1) thinking tools and (2) learning-to-learn tools. These tools should be aligned with students' developmental levels and the performance indicators and continua associated with specific impacts. Let's consider each type with examples.

Thinking Tools

Thinking tools provide students with guides to scaffold the kind of thinking needed for both disciplinary and transdisciplinary impacts. Figure 6.2 shows an example of a strategies wheel showing six problem-solving heuristics, suitable for students at the upper-elementary level. (Students in secondary schools would use a more sophisticated version.) While teachers can use such a tool to teach and model effective problem-solving strategies, its main contribution is to act as a reminder. That is, when students are working on a problem without the benefit of a teacher or another adult to guide them, the tool prompts their thinking regarding the options available.

Figure 6.3 (page 118) shows a two-part tool for helping students consider different points of view on an issue. The first presents a step-by-step process guide, while the second offers a graphic organizer for explicitly outlining and examining differing perspectives. This example is from a sixth-grade social studies unit on the settlement of the American West during the 1800s.

Similar thinking tools (such as step-by-step protocols and graphic organizers) are useful for different types of thinking, such as decision making, construction of an argument, and creative problem solving. While the example in figure 6.3 is from a sixth-grade social studies unit, the same process guide and organizer can be used for *any* issue where different points of view are likely. This point highlights the larger purpose of cognitive tools—they are intended to support *autonomous transfer* of learning to new situations, within and beyond subject areas. In fact, a basic goal of the tools is to offer students a process to use when an adult is *not* directing them.

Effective problem solvers use the following strategies when they're stuck.

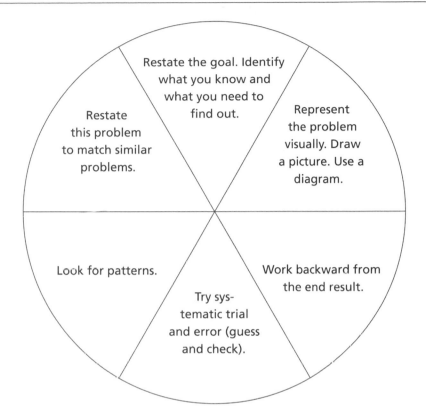

Figure 6.2: Sample problem-solving strategies wheel.

Learning-to-Learn Tools

If the development of a lifelong, self-directed learner is in your mission, then learning-to-learn tools can play a vital role in realizing this outcome. As previously discussed, we need to unpack the impact to identify the performance areas and associated performance indicators and arrange these along sets of developmental continua. Now we go a step further and also identify a set of tools aligned to both disciplinary and transdisciplinary impacts and organized by developmental stages, from simpler to more sophisticated, to support the long-term goals of 21st century learning—enabling students to transfer their learning.

Considering Different Perspectives

- Select a topic or issue to examine.

- Identify different people or groups who may be involved or affected.

- Think about how the situation might look from different vantage points.

- Consider:

    o What is another point of view on this issue?

    o What might _____ think or feel about this?

    o What is the minority position?

    o What would a devil's advocate say?

Example: Settlement of the American West

Perspective Chart

Use the following chart to examine different perspectives on an issue or topic.

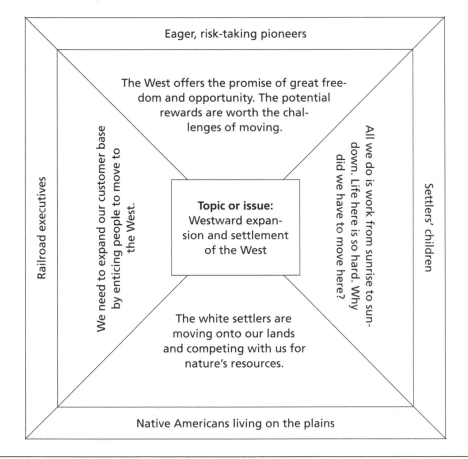

Figure 6.3: Sample process guide and graphic organizer for considering different perspectives.

Let's look at a few examples for the transdisciplinary impact of *self-directed learners*. Figure 6.4 represents the unpacking of one performance area of self-directed learning (planning and implementing plans) into performance indicators organized into a simple continuum across four grade bands with tools for each.

Impact: Self-Directed Learners			
Performance Area: Planning and Implementation			
K–2 Performance Indicators	**3–5 Performance Indicators**	**6–8 Performance Indicators**	**9–12 Performance Indicators**
• Understanding that smaller tasks should be sequenced in order to complete larger tasks	• Breaking a larger task into smaller tasks • Following steps of a plan to achieve goals	• Devising multiple work processes and timelines needed to achieve long-term goals • Adjusting plans as needs arise with a clear understanding of the nature of midcourse corrections and why they are needed	• Using specific tools and processes to stay on track • Tracking and adjusting project work processes needed to achieve long-term goals and complex tasks
Possible Tool • Sequence chain graphic organizer	Possible Tool • Simple three-part project plan (what, how, and when)	Possible Tool • Trello online project-management tool	Possible Tool • Project management software with Gantt chart or other reporting tools

Figure 6.4: Sample tools for planning and implementation.

The tools to support student development in these areas do not have to be complex or complicated. They simply need to be effective, developmentally appropriate, and part of a growing toolkit for student learning and performance in impact areas.

Figures 6.5, 6.6, and 6.7 (page 122) represent the learning-to-learn tools appropriate for the 3–5 and 6–8 grade bands in figure 6.4.

Goal or Task: Provide Fresh Water		
What are the smaller steps that need to be completed in order to achieve your goal?	**How will you accomplish this step?**	**When do we need to complete this step?**
Step: Identify the Problem	Plan: • Try to find out why people can't get fresh water. • Identify the biggest obstacles. • Clearly state the real problem.	Date: October 12
Step: Brainstorm Solutions and Select the Best One	Plan: • Use our brainstorming process to generate ideas. • Use the "idea sifter" to find out which ones might not work because of the obstacles above. • Identify the one that has the best chance of working.	Date: October 15
Step: Create the Best Solution and Sell It to the Panel	Plan: • Describe why the best idea might help solve the problem. • Look at the steps and resources needed for the best idea to be a success. • Create text, images, and some video to explain the solution and why it could solve the problem. • Put this into a presentation. • Practice and present.	Date: October 25

Figure 6.5: Sample three-part project plan tool for grades 3–5.

*Visit **go.solution-tree.com/leadership** for a reproducible version of this figure.*

Figure 6.5 is a simple and age-appropriate tool, yet it provides students with a framework for breaking down larger tasks and planning for their completion. This framework could be used across subject areas so that the process becomes natural for self-directed learners at this developmental stage when they are faced with a challenging individual or group task.

The screenshot in figure 6.6 features Trello (https://trello.com), which is one of various online planning tools that older students can use to engage in more sophisticated project planning and task tracking. Students can create cards for specific tasks and steps of the project process, assign tasks to team members, develop a checklist for each task to track completion, include a due date, upload resources, and add ongoing comments to each card. Cards can then be moved across different and customizable sections of the project board, such as the "Planned," "Doing," "Done," and "Products" cards shown here.

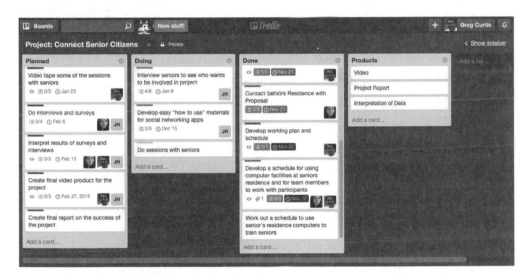

Source: Trello, Inc., 2015. Used with permission. This publication is not affiliated or associated in any way with, or endorsed in any way by, Trello, Inc.

Figure 6.6: Sample of the Trello planning tool for grades 6–8.

Figure 6.7 (page 122) is a more detailed image of a Trello card for a specific element or task within a project. Note the ability to assign team members, set due dates, track progress according to a checklist of smaller tasks, upload a document of the output of the task (in this case, a project schedule), and subscribe to a card to get notifications of changes and calendar events.

By using a consistent set of such cognitive tools over time, educators equip students to internalize the processes and strategies needed to realize desired impacts—autonomous transfer within and beyond the school.

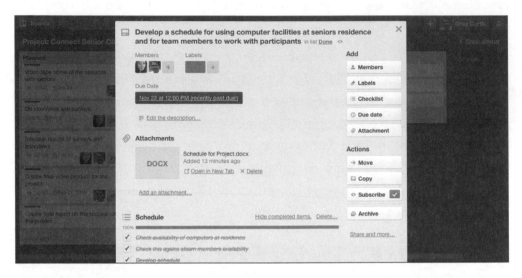

Source: Trello, Inc., 2015. Used with permission. This publication is not affiliated or associated in any way with, or endorsed in any way by, Trello, Inc.

Figure 6.7: Detail of a Trello card to support project planning and completion.

Conclusion

In this chapter, we explored ways of teaching and supporting the development of 21st century transdisciplinary impacts. We highlighted the importance of beginning with a clear articulation of principles of learning. We outlined the AMT framework and discussed appropriately matched instructional approaches. We cautioned readers to avoid confusing means and ends by rushing to adopt particular teaching methods or programs before clearly articulating desired impacts. We explored three important aspects of 21st century learning—habits of mind, technology applications, and personalized learning—and noted that the use of these approaches needs to be explicitly aligned to targeted impacts, and not simply things that we "do."

Much of our discussion has revolved around the shifts in approaches to teaching and learning that need to be made to achieve desired impacts. One such shift calls for teachers to expand their role as facilitators to help learners independently transfer their learning rather than function primarily as dispensers of content information. Accordingly, we closed the chapter by highlighting the value of cognitive tools—both thinking tools and learning-to-learn tools—that become more sophisticated over a student's career to support his or her proficiency in self-directed learning.

Our next chapter will come full circle as the alignment of all systems and processes enables us to look at reporting of students' performance and progress in a fresh and innovative manner.

CHAPTER 7

A Reporting System for Modern Learning

How do we communicate student achievement and growth of 21st century learning?

By following the backward design processes in this book, we should now have a well-aligned, mission-driven system with a focus on impacts. This focus should guide our curriculum mapping from a macro level to a micro level and align all of our assessments so they provide data to show student performance and growth in areas related to our impacts. Now we are ready to draw our work together in a manner that satisfies our original goal—to enact our vision and mission in a way that is demonstrated through student performance.

Throughout this book, we have described the important inputs of constructing a system for various outputs (curriculum, assessment, instruction, reporting, and other supportive structures), all of which are aligned with our stated impacts. It is worth pausing for a moment to retrace our journey and reiterate the major inputs that have gotten us to this stage.

1. Creating a compelling, futures-focused vision for schooling

2. Developing a mission that brings this vision to life by specifying desired impacts—the long-term transfer goals that we seek in student performance

3. Utilizing a backward design planning process to move from mission to action

4. Crafting a blueprint to guide the development of a curriculum and assessment system aligned to the mission

5. Constructing an assessment system of cornerstone tasks to evaluate student achievement and growth for both disciplinary and transdisciplinary impacts

6. Identifying instructional approaches and learning opportunities to develop the knowledge, skills, and understandings that students will need in order to demonstrate the desired achievements

A clear and compelling vision and mission are necessary but insufficient. A robust and coherent curriculum and assessment system is imperative but incomplete. And a rich and authentic teaching and learning program is vital but not the end goal. Throughout this journey, we have been careful to distinguish the inputs from the outputs. We have kept the end in mind by focusing on the long-term impacts, within and across disciplines, and by planning backward from them.

All of this work has brought us to the point where we can consolidate and document evidence of student performance and growth that aligns with our vision and mission. Now we need a constant stream of quality data on learning and performance that students, parents, teachers, administrators, and policymakers can use to assess how actual performance (at an individual, classroom, schoolwide, or districtwide level) stacks up against these sought-after impacts.

In this final chapter, we will explore ideas for transforming traditional reporting processes and products (such as report cards) into a more robust record of student accomplishment and growth on *all* of our mission-declared impacts. We will then discuss the concept of a learning board—a tangible way to put learning and student performance related to desired impacts at the heart of a school's measures of success and improvement efforts. Finally, we'll discuss various ways to collect the data necessary for a mission-based reporting system.

Report Cards: Purposes and Promises

Most schools provide periodic report cards to communicate the achievements of their students. More often than not, these reports consist of a summary mark in the form of a letter grade (A, B, C, D, F), a rubric score (4, 3, 2, 1), a symbol (VG, S, U), or a percentage for the various subject areas. While such traditional report cards are familiar to parents, students, and teachers, we believe that this common practice diminishes the value of a student's achievement by distilling all of his or her learning experiences and demonstrations of performance down to a single point or a very small number of points. Not only does a singular grade not represent the richness of student performance in the scenarios we have outlined in this book, it is also fundamentally misaligned with the type of vision and mission we have promoted.

Before we present ideas for addressing weaknesses in traditional grading and reporting practices, consider the following questions. First question—what is the purpose of a report card? Our view is that the primary goal of reporting is to communicate salient information about achievement on, and progress toward, identified impacts to students, parents, teachers, and administrators. This purpose suggests that our reports provide information on *all* of our targeted impacts—within and across disciplines. If we have identified transdisciplinary impacts in our mission, then we should report on how students are developing these capacities.

Second question—are we reporting on everything we proclaim to value? Presently, most school report cards provide a grade or rating for students' performance in academic subjects, but few effectively communicate about the achievement of mission-related impacts. Admittedly, transdisciplinary impacts such as creativity, global citizenship, and self-directed learning are more challenging to assess and grade. However, unless we evaluate and report on student performance related to these impacts, they will be seen as less important and will not receive the necessary attention. They must become part of our definition of success for our learners and schools.

Third question—what is a report card grade, and how are grades determined? A report card grade is simply a symbolic representation of some achievement or performance level. In order to function as a communication vehicle, grades must have clear meaning and be computed in a fair and consistent manner. However, a complicating factor in clear communication exists when teachers are obligated to record a *single* reporting grade for a subject area or mission-related outcome.

By averaging various factors such as achievement, improvement, and effort, the meaning of grades can be unwittingly compromised.

Finally, how can reporting be enhanced? We join other advocates of grading and reporting reform in proposing that three separate factors should be evaluated and reported: (1) achievement of impacts, (2) progress toward impacts, and (3) work habits. We'll examine each more closely.

Achievement

We believe that your organization's vision- and mission-related 21st century learning goals should have a prominent place in your assessment and reporting processes. If the assessment practices previously discussed (such as grafting) are in place, there should be plenty of student performance data on both disciplinary and transdisciplinary achievements. Thus, in addition to reporting on achievement in traditional subject areas, your reporting structures should provide an individualized picture of each student's performance in 21st century skills, such as collaboration and creative thinking, across various contexts. In so doing, you will align your impacts as stated in your mission with your reporting processes and products.

Grades and reports for student achievement will have greater clarity and meaning when they are based on:

- Clearly stated and agreed-on impacts for both academic and transdisciplinary areas

- Valid assessments of those impacts

- Consistent application of evaluation criteria (rubrics and proficiency continua) based on specific performance indicators and performance standards

Reports should also be able to distinguish among different types of learning goals. For example, does an A earned by a student who can memorize facts and pass an objective recall test imply that the student understands the material deeply and has the capacity to apply that knowledge in a new situation? Not necessarily! Indeed, most current assessment and reporting systems do not sufficiently differentiate between such substantively different measures. Thus, we propose that a finer-grained approach to reporting student achievement is needed to distinguish between the *acquisition* of foundational knowledge and skills from *application* and *transfer*. Figure 7.1 offers an example of this distinction for mathematics.

Performance Areas	Performance Indicators
Foundational Knowledge and Skills	• Knowledge of basic operations • Computational accuracy
Application and Transfer	• Application of appropriate knowledge, skills, conceptual understanding, and mathematical reasoning to solve complex, real-world problems

Source: Adapted from the International School of Beijing, 2012.

Figure 7.1: Sample distinction of goal types for seventh-grade mathematics.

Progress

Personal growth and progress toward identified impacts deserve a separate grade. Since students come to learning situations at different starting points, progress at different rates, and have varied strengths as learners, fairness demands that we communicate their degree of improvement relative to where they began (such as from the last marking period). For example, when a struggling student makes significant progress along a specified continuum, that improvement should be reported and celebrated.

Reporting on progress is natural in certain athletic endeavors, such as swimming and karate; well-developed proficiency scales enable teachers to clearly and consistently describe the performance level of an individual and set goals for the improvements needed to reach the next level. Proficiency scales are also readily available for the processes of reading, writing, listening, and speaking for English language arts and world languages. By reporting on progress separately from achievement, education becomes more personalized, and our reports become more honest and informative.

Work Habits

Productive work habits, such as completing work on time, persisting when faced with challenging tasks, participating actively, and acting on feedback, are vital capacities in school and in life. Reporting on work habits highlights the efforts of the diligent student while properly exposing the loafer. Of course, there is a need to operationally define the habits we wish to include and then identify observable performance indicators for each. For example, middle school teachers at West Windsor-Plainsboro Schools (New Jersey) developed indicators such as the following to define the attributes of a responsible, self-directed learner.

- Arrive prepared for class
- Plan and budget time to meet deadlines
- Follow through on commitments
- Attend to and follow directions
- Manage my behavior so that I remain focused
- Organize time and materials
- Persevere in challenging situations
- Take ownership of work and actions
- Strive to do my best work in all situations
- Strive for accuracy
- Undertake independent study

The specificity of these indicators enables both teachers and students to assess these habits consistently and report on them with clarity.

These recommendations for enhancing our reports reflect an axiom—what we grade and report signal what we value. By including transdisciplinary impacts along with disciplinary impacts, we signal that our mission-related outcomes really matter. By distinguishing acquisition of foundational knowledge and skills from understanding and transfer, we highlight the value of the application of learning. By reporting on progress toward impacts, we signal that we value individual growth and continuous improvement. By including work habits as a separate reporting category, we signal that such habits are important to success and are respected.

The Learning Board Concept

Traditional report cards are time bound and tied to the school calendar. At certain increments (often after a flurry of reporting deadline assessments), the school will churn out a report. However, what if we saw reporting as an opportunity to communicate student progress at the most auspicious times (which may vary by class, subject, and grade level) rather than by reporting only on arbitrary dates? What if reports included products of student learning that are interpreted against stated goals, past performance trends, and unique, personalized demonstrations of performance?

It is our contention that evidence of modern learning can and should be captured, packaged, and delivered through a much more robust reporting system than currently exists in most schools. We can still deliver traditional grades, but we need a sophisticated and multifaceted set of metrics to authentically report on all of the student accomplishments declared in our mission.

One way to visualize such a reporting system is through a digital tool known as a *learning board*. Think of a learning board as a digital dashboard that captures evidence of student learning (both process and product), organizes this evidence around the desired impacts, and allows students, parents, teachers, and administrators to interact with this data using sophisticated analytic tools. We have worked with the educational software company EduTect to develop such a system, commercially known as LearningBoard.

This system, which can capture, aggregate, and interpret learning data around the school's mission and impacts, offers:

- A real-time reporting dashboard that stores and communicates performance reports dynamically (such as on student achievement, progress, and work habits)

- An extended e-portfolio system that stores results from assessments, examples of student work, and student self-assessments

- A simple learning management system (LMS) that facilitates access to the curriculum and related resources and enables learning transactions (teacher-student, student-student, and student-parent)

- An integrated gradebook with criteria and performance indicators linked to assessments (such as cornerstone tasks)

- Infographics to communicate achievement of disciplinary and transdisciplinary learning, progress, and work habits

- A dynamic picture of student learning, available 24-7 to students, parents, and educators

- Tools for students to use for project planning, self-assessment, reflection, goal setting, and housing personalized artifacts of their learning

Consider how such a resource could significantly enhance the quality and quantity of communication about student performance and growth relative to a school's mission. Teachers could include a broader array of evidence to communicate about student learning. They could bundle data from multiple sources, including classroom assessments, standardized tests, artifacts contributed by learners (captured through cell phones and tablets within the learning environment), and student self-assessments and reflections. Such a collection of evidence could be different for each student, allowing individuals to demonstrate achievement and growth in a more personal manner. Moreover, a report can be issued when it is most natural and timely, such as at the end of a unit or a major project rather than only at fixed times.

A great deal of learning in a modern learning environment (especially in the area of transdisciplinary impacts) can be demonstrated as students work on authentic tasks and projects. It is artificial and unnecessary to ask students to stop what they are doing so teachers can assess them in a decontextualized manner. Just as athletic coaches assess the players' performance in a game, a learning board system would enable teachers to capture students' demonstrations of impacts in the context of genuine performances.

While this type of reporting may seem like a lot of work for the teacher, we encourage you to think of it as a repurposing of existing time by using efficient technologies. For example, teachers are already recording grades and preparing reports; we simply shift this task into a more dynamic assessment and reporting environment. If curriculum information is pulled directly from an existing source (such as a curriculum-mapping system), we eliminate the need to maintain a class website within an LMS to provide basic curriculum information, calendar items, assignments, and resources. This could create added efficiencies that allow us to trade that time for capturing evidence of learning *in situ* and sharing with students.

If such evidence of student learning is captured, tagged, and interpreted with explicit alignment to clear impacts, we can develop an extremely rich picture of evolving growth and accomplishment, especially when students contribute relevant evidence of their learning drawn from a variety of experiences and venues.

Ted's LearningBoard

Let's now look at an example of EduTect's LearningBoard for a hypothetical student named Ted to envision the possibilities. Ted and his classmates have been tasked with showing their understanding of a specific book by compiling various sources of evidence. For this assignment, Ted knows that he needs to provide an artifact, a self-assessment, and a reflection on the meaning of the book. For his artifact, Ted decides to create a short video trailer for a hypothetical movie version of the book to display his understanding as well as to showcase his developing communication skills. For his self-assessment and reflection, Ted uses a developed rubric to self-assess his understanding of the book and records an audio commentary on his cell phone to reflect on its meaning. He uploads both the video and audio files to his LearningBoard.

This example illustrates the potential of collecting evidence from multiple sources, not just from static, moment-in-time tests. As learning environments become more personalized, we should not assume that all meaningful learning is confined to the classroom or the school calendar. Indeed, the use of LearningBoard could allow students to contribute evidence and reflections from learning experiences that take place outside of traditional school hours. Students should be able to provide evidence of performance from summer programs, work experiences, participation in clubs and sports, family travel, and related personal events that demonstrate learning and performance in areas related to stated impacts. They should be able to send an artifact to a mentor outside of the school for commentary and assessment and incorporate this feedback.

We believe that we need to prepare for a new era of personalization in which students have greater control of the direction and form of their learning. As schooling becomes personalized and "anytime, anywhere" learning becomes more of a reality, resources like LearningBoard will be essential to capture the totality of learning experiences and help educators, parents, and students interpret these experiences in light of desired impacts and related performance indicators.

Figure 7.2 depicts a sample of Ted's LearningBoard home screen, showing various display categories and available tools.

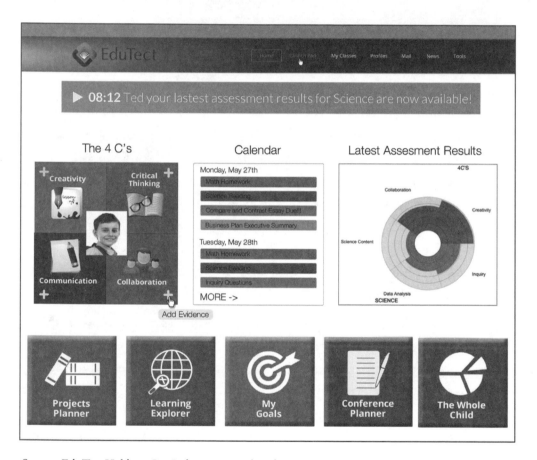

Source: EduTect Holdings Pty Ltd, 2015. Used with permission.

Figure 7.2: LearningBoard home screen.

Performance Tracking

Students (and their parents) should be able to track performance over time in order to set realistic goals and move forward. Doing so allows learners to reflect on their learning and gain a better understanding of where they are and where they need to be in various disciplinary and transdisciplinary areas. In the Latest Assessment Results section of LearningBoard (upper right of figure 7.2), Ted's performance on his most recent assessment is displayed. It shows performance data in an interactive circumplex that allows the viewer to drill down to see the actual evidence sources and gain useful insights from these snapshots of achievement. Such a feature places the freshest data in front of Ted so that he has immediate access to feedback on his work in a particular area. He can also compare his latest performance with previous attempts and combine data from different assignments and assessments. This data display can also help Ted's teachers know how to adjust instruction to better support his learning.

Assessing and reporting on transdisciplinary impacts can often be more challenging than grading the attainment of traditional subject matter. Moreover, mission-based transdisciplinary impacts are more likely to differ from school to school, so a customizable learning board system will be needed. As an example, let's look at the relevant components of Ted's screen to see how his school measures each student's progress toward three transdisciplinary impacts it chose to focus on: (1) the 4Cs of 21st century learning (critical thinking, creativity, collaboration, and communication); (2) traits and attributes of well-rounded and principled contributors to society; and (3) skills, traits, and attributes of self-directed learners.

The 4Cs area of Ted's LearningBoard illustrated in figure 7.3 (page 136) acts as a clearinghouse for all evidence of learning that reflects student performance and achievement related to the 4Cs performance indicators. The bar graph displays his demonstration of skills in critical thinking, collaboration, communication, and creativity within various subject areas, while the balance wheel shows his composite performance in these 4Cs.

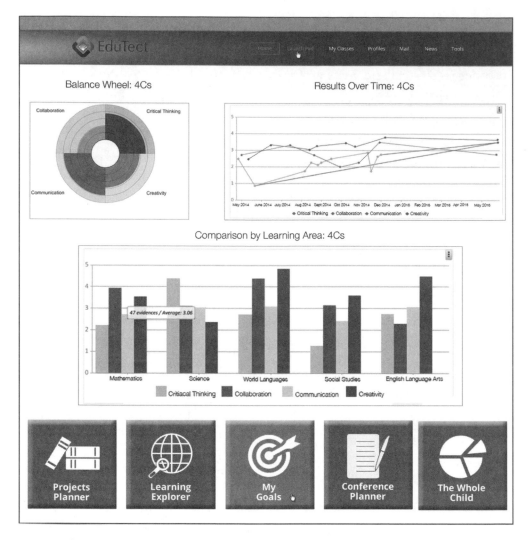

Source: EduTect Holdings Pty Ltd, 2015. Used with permission.

Figure 7.3: Example of the 4Cs area of Ted's LearningBoard.

All performance data from assessments and cornerstone tasks to which the 4Cs were grafted are available here, along with other student-contributed artifacts of learning aligned with performance indicators. Students would be expected to self-assess these artifacts using the same criteria and rubrics as teachers use to assess performance. Student reflections on evidence captured during learning (by the student, a peer, or the teacher) would also be aligned with transdisciplinary impacts and be self- or peer-assessed. For instance, Ted can self-assess his video of a group interaction that occurred during a service-learning experience against performance indicators in the area of collaboration. All of these data are consolidated in the interactive graphic at the top left of the 4Cs screen. Users can drill down to look at individual pieces of evidence and their contribution to that larger performance and growth picture.

The results at the top right of figure 7.3 show how performance from all three types of evidence can be aggregated in a custom "change over time" graph. Each node on the graph represents a piece of evidence. Clicking on a node provides access to that particular piece of evidence along with whatever teacher assessment, self-assessment, comment, reflection, and artifact is included. The comparison graph below it simply shows another way for Ted to view his performance in the 4Cs across various learning areas. He can generate questions about his performance across various disciplines that may lead to valuable insights.

Note that Ted or his parents can make quick observations on a holistic level and then do a deeper dive into a particular area to learn more. By promoting this sort of inquiry, we hope to engage students in reflecting on their ongoing performance and support them in making observations, generating insights, and targeting areas needing improvement.

Project Planning and Management

A growing number of schools interested in developing 21st century skills have instituted project-based learning (PBL) as a means of engaging students in more active and authentic learning. PBL demands that learners increase their capacity to plan and manage their time and actions without excessive teacher direction. LearningBoard offers tools for students to use in the design, implementation, and monitoring of projects and long-term assignments.

For example, in the Projects Planner area of LearningBoard, Ted can propose a project-based inquiry, use project management tools to organize his approach and those of his teammates, share resources, review benchmarks, and coordinate his project through its various stages. By providing such real-world planning and tracking tools to manage projects, the system contributes to the development of self-directed and collaborative learners.

Conferencing

At various stages, students will need to organize evidence of learning for an audience. That audience may be their parents (student-led conferences), teachers (facilitator conferences), or even people from outside the school (exhibitions, presentations to experts, internships, or mentor conferences). Planning and conducting periodic conferences help students compile and present authentic evidence of achievement and growth to an audience, thereby assuming greater ownership of their learning.

Through LearningBoard, Ted has access to a Conference Planner to support his organization of evidence and presentation of his overall performance and growth. In essence, Ted can create a series of "best of Ted" snapshots to use for various conferencing opportunities and audiences.

Goal Setting

Setting goals supports the ongoing development of metacognitive and self-directed learning skills. Students need to be able to develop queries and break down their performances in multiple ways to help them gain insights into their learning. The key is to make all of this rich performance data available and organized in easily accessible and understandable formats (such as infographics) that can help students truly understand their learning strengths and areas needing greater attention.

In the My Goal section of LearningBoard, Ted can access his collected performance evidence, thus allowing him to make observations, draw inferences, and look for trends. These data become the basis for his goal setting. He can track progress toward his goals by consolidating evidence dynamically and authentically. In fact, these analytics run through all sections and provide students with age-appropriate tools to follow their individual growth and any related evidence. For example, Ted may want to compare his performance in critical thinking in mathematics and science with his performance in the same impact area in social studies and English. He might ask, "Does my performance vary in areas that require different types of critical thinking? If so, how? And why?" Or perhaps he wants to know, "How has my performance in the 4Cs changed over time?" Or, "Did my performance in collaboration improve once I tried to use some of the collaborative strategies I learned?"

Student-Contributed Evidence

Portfolios, including digital versions, have been around for many years as compendia of various pieces of student work. However, too often, these collections exist outside the mainstream learning environment and represent a compilation without interpretation. While we certainly endorse the value of collecting and compiling evidence of student work, it is important that these contributions align with articulated learning goals and the indicators of performance and growth tied to the desired impacts. Work samples need to align with teacher assessments to provide complementary evidence of a student's learning story.

LearningBoard enables learners to contribute artifacts as evidence of their learning and growth. It supports students' self-assessment, reflection, and goal setting in a manner that reinforces self-directed learning. Figure 7.4 shows the Evidence area of Ted's LearningBoard.

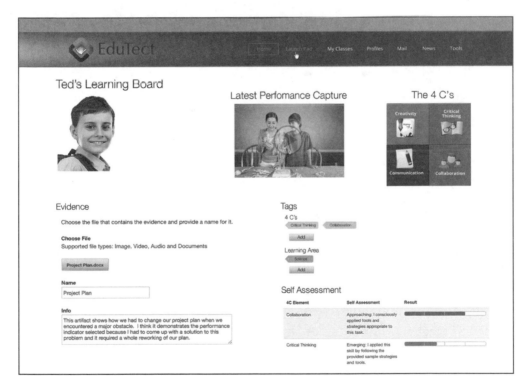

Source: EduTect Holdings Pty Ltd, 2015. Used with permission.

Figure 7.4: Example of the artifacts and evidence area of Ted's LearningBoard.

In this example, Ted has contributed artifacts (a project plan and a video clip). Ted can then place these particular artifacts within a context (such as part of a learning activity or unit assessment) and tag them as such. Ted can add a commentary about the artifacts and what he believes they reflect. Finally, he can tag them as being representative of his performance or growth in the 4Cs and self-assess his performance based on a common assessment rubric and descriptors also used by his teachers. His contributions can be compared with teacher assessments in similar areas.

Student-contributed artifacts such as these can be aligned to both academic goals and transdisciplinary impacts. Artifacts and evidence of learning can be tagged with performance indicators that represent the observable skills and actions of self-directed learners. They can be tracked over time as evidence of progress toward a goal and can be included in a new form of "report card" that values student input as part of the central story of their learning.

The Whole Child

The Whole Child area of LearningBoard allows Ted to contribute artifacts from experiences outside of school that represent his growth across multiple impacts. For example, feedback from a summer job could be contributed as evidence of his collaborative skills. Other evidence from extracurricular activities, clubs, hobbies, and personal interests can be collected and compiled on LearningBoard. In this way, the value of transdisciplinary impacts is elevated even as the importance of cultivating whole-child development is reinforced.

Teacher and Parent Data Collection

LearningBoard allows teachers and administrators to access, analyze, and use data in countless ways. Each piece of evidence has multiple relationships with students, teachers, subject areas, grades, impacts, and so on, and all of these relationships can be fruitfully mined by aggregating and disaggregating learning data. For example, a teacher might like to look at a particular student, such as Ted, and see whether he has shown the same levels of performance in the 4Cs in other classes or grade levels. Maybe the teacher wants to compare her class's 4Cs performance on a cornerstone task with that of other classes.

As part of a professional learning community (PLC), a team of teachers could use their analysis of various data sources for both disciplinary and transdisciplinary impacts to target areas of student learning needing improvement. They could introduce tools or strategies to address deficit areas and track changes over time to see if these inputs and outputs have had the desired impact.

Parents should also have access to data on their child's achievement and progress, including work products and self-assessments. For instance, Ted's parents could apply simple analytic tools to gain insights about Ted's learning strengths and areas needing attention. This level of access and transparency means that the school's mission and its definition of success permeate the entire community and are strengthened on all fronts.

While the concept is relatively simple, the alignment of all systems is very powerful when it focuses on documenting the achievement of a mission through tangible, concrete evidence drawn from many rich sources of student performance.

A Day in the Life

The ideas we have put forward in this chapter may be difficult to visualize since they depart from familiar school reporting practices. They could easily be viewed as an amalgamation of existing tools, such as electronic gradebooks, data dashboards, e-portfolios, learning management systems, and the like. Perhaps the best way to understand how our concepts not only integrate these elements but also amplify and align them with impacts to enhance learning is through an illustrative narrative. So consider a "day in the life" of a middle school student and how she interacts with her LearningBoard. (As previously noted, this narrative is a good example of a futures artifact that could be developed to tell the story of a school's preferred future and vision for learning.)

Kelly arrives at school on a Tuesday morning. After chatting with her friends, she enters class and opens her laptop. She notices a few messages; several are all-class announcements, but one is from her project facilitator reminding her group about their meeting later that day. Another is from one of her team members on the same project, asking to meet at lunch to prepare for this check-in meeting. There is also a calendar notification of a scheduled assessment in mathematics tomorrow morning.

Kelly opens up her LearningBoard and sees that there are new assessment results available for the presentation she did in science the day before. She looks at her grade; any comments about foundations, application, and transfer; and her impact areas of communication and critical thinking. She looks at the photo of her presenting her project on ecosystems and reads the teacher's comments about the effective way she presented the supporting data for her solution. She looks at her marks across all areas and thinks to herself, "It looks like I didn't back up my idea enough, so I'll have to work on that next time."

As class begins, the teacher asks students to go to a recent artifact they have submitted for one of the 4Cs and share that through LearningBoard with the person to their left. That student will respond by making comments online; then the two students will engage in a mini-conference about their specific artifact and what it demonstrates for five minutes. The students then switch roles and begin another mini-conference.

Kelly goes to a recent artifact she uploaded—the comparison chart she did in social studies as evidence of critical thinking—and shares it with Anika, the girl to her left. In turn, she receives notification that William, the boy to her right, has shared an artifact with her. She opens the artifact tagged as an example of collaboration, reads William's comment, and then adds her own, along with an evaluation of the extent to which William demonstrated the performance indicators he selected on the associated performance continuum. She meets with Anika to discuss her interpretations and then with William to share her own.

After a brief introduction to the mathematics activity for the morning, the teacher directs everyone to the unit resources for this activity on their screens. Kelly and her partner sit together, review the activity and the resources, and get to work on the mathematics challenge. During the activity, using a school iPad, Kelly snaps a photo of the bridge they were constructing—after it collapsed under less than the required weight. She shares the photo with her partner digitally. Later, she will go back and tag the photo as evidence of *learning from failure* in the list of traits of a self-directed learner and add a comment about what they learned from that failure and how they changed their approach in the subsequent attempt. She probably won't assess herself very highly on this performance indicator, since they skipped adjusting their plan and calculations first and instead went forward in a trial-and-error manner.

At lunch, Kelly sits with her project partner to prepare for their check-in with their facilitator later in the day. They review their project plan and complete a few unfinished elements that they realize need to be included in the Project Planner. They plan to share these changes with their facilitator.

The day ends, as it always does, with a group session with her learning coach. The coach reminds them that feedback has been provided for their performance in the just-completed social studies unit.

"Tonight," the coach says, "I'd like you to review the feedback and add your self-assessments and comments alongside the performance summary for the whole unit. Review the evidence your teacher has provided for your learning during this unit, and try to refer to it in your comments. The feedback will be available to your parents to view on Thursday, so please complete this tonight for review tomorrow."

Finally, they are all given some time to use as they wish. Some of Kelly's classmates upload, tag, self-assess, and comment on an artifact. Some go to the Conference Planner section and organize a few pieces of evidence for their student-led conference at the beginning of next week. Kelly checks the progress on the goal she has set around creative thinking, and she knows she has received some assessment results that include performance indicators for this impact from the past couple of weeks. She reruns her query to look at her teachers' assessments for all performance indicators in this area and looks for change over time. She is pleased to see that her performance in this area seems to be improving across her classes, and she adds a reflection stating that she believes her use of some of the idea-generating tools and processes has helped her improvement.

Kelly reviews her tasks for the evening and makes some notes in her journal about what she needs to do in a few areas. The bell rings, and Kelly and her friends hurry for the bus.

Conclusion

If we take our mission seriously, we must evaluate and report on our progress toward achieving it. All sources of evidence must align with impacts, and students, teachers, and parents should interpret student learning according to the performance indicators representative of these impacts. With this depth of alignment, everyone involved can follow cohort groups across departments, schools, or districts to track progress toward desired impacts on multiple levels (individual, cohort, department, school, or district) at any point in time and in multiple ways.

This is also where the Input-Output-Impact framework returns. Implementing change efforts by focusing on inputs and outputs rarely helps a learning organization realize its aspirational goals. Working from a desired end, however, can serve as a unifier for progressive efforts within a school. Up to this point, we have used the framework to work backward to plan inputs and outputs aligned with stated impacts as a way to carry out implementation. Here, the IOI framework can also be used to evaluate the progress and success of our strategic initiatives on a systemic scale.

Through systems like LearningBoard, we can explore correlations among inputs, outputs, and successes or failures at achieving impacts. Which actions, innovations, program implementations, processes, tools, and so on have contributed to success or failure? How do we maximize the approaches that worked (that we believe contributed to progress toward impact) and eliminate or redirect initiatives that didn't? In other words, how do we use multiple sources of data to become more adaptive and focused on continuous improvement in order to achieve our impacts and, therefore, deliver on our mission?

Any reporting and alignment approach should be flexible and customizable enough to align with an individual school's or district's unique vision and mission for 21st century learning. Data-collection and reporting tools are only as good as the work that precedes them and the alignment of all elements across the system. Having said that, we have also seen how systems like LearningBoard can help drive desired changes backward through these systems.

The ways in which a department, school, or district captures, organizes, and communicates student learning say a lot about what it really values. We often see schools where there is little, if any, alignment between their missions and the ways in which they assess and report student performance. There is a big difference between attending to your mission and achieving it. This point, we believe, brings our book full circle. We started with the need to develop a compelling 21st century vision for learning and an actionable mission based on desired impacts. We now conclude with a potential resolution to the dilemma of how learning organizations can point to evidence of achievement of their visions and missions.

Executing the processes outlined in this book will, no doubt, seem daunting. This is long-term work. But we believe that when taken step by step, these elements are achievable and necessary to bring a level of alignment and intentionality to living out your vision and mission for modern learning.

Our focus is not on *what* you should become but rather on *how* you can achieve the future you seek for your students. We hope that the steps outlined in this book will help you take on this future with purpose and confidence.

Sources for Futures-Oriented Thinking Tools and Processes

Organizations around the world have done and are doing much work in the area of futures-oriented thinking in education. This is work that most schools are not equipped to undertake on their own; thus, these materials can substantially help these schools build a knowledge base and move from insights to foresights as part of the processes outlined in chapter 1. (Visit **go.solution-tree .com/leadership** to access materials related to this book.)

- **Futurelab:** www.futurelab.org.uk

- **Institute for the Future:** www.iftf.org

- **KnowledgeWorks:** http://knowledgeworks.org

- **MindShift:** http://blogs.kqed.org/mindshift

- **New Zealand Council for Educational Research:** www.nzcer.org.nz

- **Organisation for Economic Co-operation and Development:** www.oecd.org/site/schoolingfortomorrowknowledgebase /futuresthinking/futuresthinking.htm

Sources to Develop Performance Indicators for the 4Cs

Following are examples and resources for developing performance indicators, continua, and rubrics. This list is designed to be illustrative, not exclusionary or comprehensive. Many resources exist to support this work, and we encourage departments, schools, and districts to find sources relevant and useful to them. We've compiled these resources as merely a sample of the great work being done in these areas. (Visit **go.solution-tree.com/leadership** to access materials related to this book.)

Please remember to acknowledge the work of others, and cite all sources used in your processes!

The 4Cs

- **EdLeader21's 4Cs rubrics:** www.edleader21.com/order.php

Critical Thinking

- **Department of Defense Education Activity's reflection and evaluation rubrics (also includes other 21st century skills):** https://content.dodea.edu/VS/21st_century/web/21/21_skills _reflection_evaluation_rubrics.html

- **National Education Association's** *Preparing 21st Century Students for a Global Society* **guide (includes links to resources for most 21st century skills as well):** www.nea.org/assets/docs/A-Guide-to -Four-Cs.pdf

Creativity

- **Grant Wiggins's "On Assessing for Creativity: Yes You Can, and Yes You Should" handout (includes a link to creativity assessment ideas and a rubric):** https://grantwiggins.wordpress. com/2012/02/03 /on-assessing-for-creativity-yes-you-can-and-yes-you-should

- **State of Washington Office of Superintendent of Public Instruction's 21st century skills standards rubrics (includes other 21st century skills rubrics):** www.k12.wa.us/careerteched /pubdocs/21stcenturyskillsstandardsrubric.doc

- **Susan Brookhart's rubric for creativity:** www.ascd.org/publications /educational-leadership/feb13/vol70/num05/Assessing-Creativity.aspx

Collaboration

- **Buck Institute for Education's collaboration rubrics (other CCSS-aligned and non-CCSS rubrics available as well):** http://bie.org /results/search&keywords=collaboration+rubric&category=

- **Catalina Foothills School District's Envision21 Deep Learning collaboration rubric for grades K–2 (other rubrics are also available):** www.cfsd16.org/public/_century/pdf/Rubrics /Collaboration.pdf

- **Howard-Suamico School District's 21st century skills rubrics (other rubrics also available):** http://hssd21.weebly.com/21st -century-skills-rubrics.html

Communication

- **Future of Education wiki's 21st century skills sample rubrics:** https://future-of-education.wikispaces.com/21st+Century+Skills +Sample+Rubrics

- **Saywire's 21st century learning objectives rubric (includes other 21st century skills):** https://saywire.com/downloads/21st-Century -Learning-Objectives-Rubric.pdf

APPENDIX C

Sample Performance Indicators for 21st Century Skills

The following figure is meant to serve as an example of a performance indicator continuum that could be developed around the skills related to a school's transdisciplinary impacts. It is not meant to be comprehensive; rather, it is included as an example of the type of unpacking that schools can undertake. For ease of reference, the 21st century skills are listed in alphabetical order.

Collaboration

Performance Area	Elementary	Middle	High
Elevates the work of others through collaborative processes and task-management skills	• Breaks a larger task into smaller tasks and shares these across the team • Follows steps of team plan to achieve goals • Identifies the skills that individuals bring to the team • Shows emerging self-management to stay focused	• Develops and follows group norms for group processes • Structures team tasks to maximize the talents and experience of individual team members • Helps develop a high level of trust and reciprocity • Adjusts plans as needs arise with a clear understanding of the nature of midcourse corrections and why they are needed • Uses tools and processes to aid work	• Uses group norms and facilitation processes to build on the successes or challenges of individuals • Sequences tasks to build on each other in a value-added way • Takes on distinct roles as a team member, even when team hierarchy is relatively flat • Uses specific tools and processes to keep on track and pursue solutions
Builds on the learning and ideas of others	• Initiates discussion of group learning and ideas • Brainstorms and sifts through simple ideas to approach the task or problem • Asks questions to clarify understanding of others' ideas • Engages in back-and-forth or give-and-take dialogue	• Advances and stimulates discussion of group learning and ideas • Extrapolates on the learning of others and connects this with the task • Acts on the perspectives of others and uses these to broaden understanding	• Synthesizes and consolidates group learning and ideas to help create new understandings or approaches • Helps the team adjust its direction based on what has been learned • Seeks out perspectives that may differ from own • Commits to iterative nature of designing and redesigning solutions
Is a good team member	• Engages in positive group interaction • Seeks ideas and thoughts from all team members • Performs an identified role with focus • Explains own thinking and ideas clearly (continued)	• Understands and acts on the notion of collective interest as opposed to self-interest • Promotes and sustains positive group interactions (continued)	• Manages the tension between self and others • Attends to the dynamic of the group and ensures that all voices are heard • Changes role as needed to support others (continued)

	Elementary	Middle	High
	• Values the perspectives of others and understands that different viewpoints on the task or problem will exist within the team • Avoids sticking stubbornly to own perspective • Demonstrates respect and recognizes the feelings of others • Understands and commits to the shared goals of the group	• Acts with sensitivity to the value of individuals within the team dynamic • Takes positions as appropriate to the circumstances • Performs a wide range of roles within a team • Attends to the individuals in the group, not just the group as a single entity	• Seeks feedback on task and performance • Takes positions to help the group and brings in unrepresented positions • Is sensitive to the impact of context (such as virtual versus face-to-face environments) on interactions with others • Relates to and connects with others for the purpose of leading or empowering

Communication

Performance Area	Elementary	Middle	High
Communicates effectively in a multimodal world	• Engages with and can choose from various modes of communication • Explores conventions and forms of communication across modes • Uses the mode of communication best suited to the purpose and audience • Adds effectiveness and impact to communication through the inclusion of graphics and multimedia • Communicates beyond the barriers of a normal classroom through multimedia, electronic devices, email, and the Internet	• Applies conventions and forms of communication across modes • Moves between modes with dexterity, in both expressive and interpretive capacities • Selects appropriate mode by critically assessing potential options and the effectiveness of each for a particular purpose, context, and audience • Uses a range of media and technology tools (such as text, images, and design elements) strategically and in ways that add value to the product	• Moves intuitively between modes and mixes them effectively • Uses a range of media and technology tools strategically and in ways that make every aspect of the product appear well thought out, purposeful, and necessary • Identifies, joins, and regularly interacts with communities of interest and is involved in formal and informal learning through such communications • Manipulates and experiments with conventions and forms of communication across modes

continued →

Figure C.1: Sample performance indicator continuum.

Communication

Performance Area	Elementary	Middle	High
Develops powerful narrative to explain complex ideas and move people	• Arranges the parts of communication to convey ideas and information in a narrative • Arranges and enhances images and other media elements so they effectively tell a story • Sequences ideas and events to move the audience smoothly through the communication from beginning to end • Communicates with empathy and caring that connects to audiences	• Communicates information with logic and coherence in a way that leads the audience through the desired narrative • Communicates empathetically to connect people to the narrative • Connects ideas to the emotions and aspirations of audience • Uses examples, analogies, and metaphors through multiple modes to connect the audience to the narrative	• Connects audience with narrative by eliciting emotional, psychological, physical, and cognitive responses • Understands the social-emotional context (values, concerns, interests, and expectations) of the communication and tunes narrative appropriately • Spreads ideas and inspires action through powerful use of narrative
Contributes within interpretative and expressive processes	• Observes and interprets multiple modes of information • Draws logical inferences and conclusions based on communication • Uses features, conventions, and etiquette of interactive communications environments • Organizes and expresses ideas and information for others • Uses open, probing, and clarifying questions to elevate understanding of a communication product	• Contributes as an interactive member of communication processes in various arenas • Interprets abstract visuals and creates products (such as digital storytelling) that reflect a growing understanding of visual language and require the effective use of tools • Explores, probes, and clarifies information, opinions, and proposals as an active interpreter • Communicates interpretation and understanding of products clearly	• Creates information using advanced skills in analysis, synthesis, and evaluation • Engages others as an active interpreter of communication, especially in interpersonal contexts • Critically interprets all modes of communication (text, verbal, nonverbal, visual, multimedia, infographics and statistics, and so on) for meaning and validity • Communicates interpretation and understanding of products with a knowledge of medium, context, and embedded message

Critically and aesthetically analyzes the messages and stories presented	• Identifies the emotional message implicit in communication • Analyzes the context that specific communications came from • Interprets abstract visuals and mixed-media content that reflect a growing understanding of visual and media language • Interprets the relative importance of the messages we encounter • Explores the aesthetic value of products from many sources and contexts	• Gains a perspective for the source of communication and develops empathetic awareness • Understands the interdependence between culture and communication • Analyzes messages embedded within the communication encountered • Seeks to understand powerful, evocative messages without passively absorbing them • Evaluates the value of a product of communication based on aesthetic knowledge and sensibilities • Identifies own reactions and interpretations to images and the reasons behind these responses	• Identifies and appreciates the impact of design elements and techniques • Applies well-thought-out, insightful standards for gauging quality of a communication product • Elevates thinking through critical and knowledgeable interpretation • Applies critical faculties to gain insights through interpretation • Analyzes and interprets visuals and recognizes the impact media techniques and influences have on audiences
Samples, mixes, and repurposes information into new forms of communication	• Uses knowledge and tools to construct new knowledge and products • Applies creative capacities to combining source media and information • Repurposes media elements across modes in an additive manner	• Creates narrative and meaning by combining content from various sources • Develops unique perspectives through the creative mixing of elements • Repurposes media elements across modes in an integrative manner	• Engages in synthetic thought (effectively creating a product from various sources) with the materials and media with which he or she interacts • Connects with audience by mixing elements that have a shared meaning and importance

continued →

Creative Thinking

Performance Area	Elementary	Middle	High
Understands the context of the issue	• Seeks to understand the reasons for an issue or problem • Articulates ideas that are connected to context or information • Demonstrates a consideration of multiple perspectives	• Seeks to understand the elements, obvious and unapparent, of an issue or problem • Adapts responses to fit the situation • Begins to consider other perspectives • Breaks an open-ended problem into component parts relevant to the context	• Demonstrates an understanding of ethics, usefulness, and concrete applicability of an idea within a context • Actively seeks multiple perspectives and looks at information nonjudgmentally and without bias • Makes connections among contextual information, ideas, or experiences that were previously unconnected • Articulates new and evolving responses to varying situations over time
Applies flexible ways of thinking	• Demonstrates openness and originality in creating new things • Makes unusual associations and provides a variety of solutions to problems • Uses existing ideas to create new ideas • Generates ideas for solutions to problems and asks questions in order to create unusual, unique, or clever products • Uses materials, knowledge, or techniques in nontraditional ways • Uses divergent thinking to generate ideas	• Thinks of all the possibilities and divergences to become more expansive with thoughts and ideas leading to the creation of original products • Shares or advocates thinking that deviates from convention • Adapts, improves, modifies, and expands existing thoughts or ideas to create products • Is prompted to spontaneous exploration by accidental discovery • Uses inference to generate ideas and implications • Uses analysis as a tool to become creative (continued)	• Generates lists of ideas as a way of thinking • Demonstrates an increased level of sophistication and an ability to evaluate and discuss why one idea has greater merit than another • Lets discovery, exploration, and spontaneity take him or her in new directions • Generates multiple possibilities as a result of inference • Visualizes the connections between seemingly unrelated ideas and independently produces solutions that are fresh, unique, original, and well developed (continued)

	• Reorganizes seemingly disparate or disconnected ideas into like categories • Looks and thinks from multiple perspectives	• Synthesizes divergent perspectives into original thoughts
Thrives in challenging environments	• Demonstrates creativity within the framework of personalized projects • Expresses interest in and wonder at new phenomena and desires to actively pursue such interests • Demonstrates curiosity and eagerness to resolve or eliminate ambiguity • Begins to take small risks for things that are important to him or her • Sees mistakes as learning opportunities • Understands that dilemmas do not have obvious or linear solutions	• Reacts positively to novel elements in the environment • Engages in discovery, exploration, and experimentation to reach unexpected answers • Demonstrates awareness of ambiguity within an issue, an ability to infer from implication, and an ability to make reasoned and supported guesses • Embraces debate to resolve ambiguity • Uses multiple sources to help resolve ambiguity • Feels empowered, not frustrated, by having freedom to try something new • Jumps out of comfort zone in a safe environment • Responds to ill-defined situations with spontaneity	• Tackles challenging problems without obvious solutions, despite potential for failure • Gains intrinsic motivation from risks and challenges • Embraces complexity and uses it as a creative design parameter • Changes focus and goals as the situation demands • Realizes that a problem can be an opportunity to improve the overall human condition • Responds to open-ended or ill-defined situations with spontaneity and ingenuity that lead to the discovery and exploration of new ideas • Is comfortable with ambiguous meaning • Uses ambiguity as an opportunity to create something new

continued →

Creative Thinking

Performance Area	Elementary	Middle	High
Is able to process a potential design or innovation	• Begins to understand the complexity of feasibility in realizing ideas • Visualizes an idea through to completion • Creates and tests prototypes of ideas and products • Explores the intended and potential unintended consequences of solutions and designs • Identifies an application for an idea in the real world	• Analyzes the feasibility of an idea, solution, or product • Anticipates obstacles in bringing an idea to life • Uses models, prototypes, and simulations to explore complex systems and issues and propose solutions or ideas • Applies originality, concentration, commitment to completion, and persistence to develop unique and cogent products	• Takes a sophisticated idea and breaks it into parts in order to realize it in the world • Seeks resources to mitigate limitations • Understands how to be creative within set parameters, frameworks, or structures • Anticipates and develops strategies to overcome obstacles • Extrapolates from prototyping experiences to develop a highly refined solution, idea, or product

Critical Thinking

Performance Area	Elementary	Middle	High
Recognizes and works with patterns	• Poses problems and asks questions about how things work and why things happen • Recognizes patterns in the natural and human worlds • Makes applicable observations about patterns • Derives meaning from inquiring into patterns	• Recognizes similarities across patterns and makes generalizations • Identifies details, data, features, and processes that represent patterns • Classifies data, findings, and opinions using a given classification schema to look for patterns • Makes predictions based on patterns	• Identifies relevant differences, similarities, and patterns in findings • Recognizes similarities across disparate patterns and designs principles to describe them • Extrapolates and generalizes to identify patterns • Formulates categories or distinctions to understand patterns

Applies different approaches to different scenarios	• Uses models and visual representations to assist in critical thinking • Understands the basic elements of and approaches to critical thought (such as observation, comparison, analysis, evaluation, explanation, and simple reasoning processes) • Selects the critical approach that best suits the context and the inquiry • Understands that different disciplines approach critical tasks in different ways	• Identifies more open-ended problems and adapts approaches accordingly • Applies creative-thinking approaches to explore unobvious pathways • Applies appropriate disciplinary thinking to specific scenarios • Uses complex models, analogies, and simulations appropriately • Applies appropriate elements of and approaches to critical thought (such as inference, generalization, validity tests, and so on)	• Separates the problem from the context in order to more fully understand both • Connects seemingly unrelated ideas in complex scenarios to better understand them • Transfers thinking abilities to unfamiliar or novel situations • Recognizes the appropriate reasoning approach to apply within the specific context
Applies a critical eye	• Uses observation and inquiry to guide action and solve problems in deliberate ways • Distinguishes among fact, opinion, and value statements • Identifies irrelevant information • Finds an example or distinction that helps explain something • Uses observation, compare and contrast, deduction, induction, and reasoning • Identifies information and organizes it into appropriate categories (fact, inference, concept, opinion, experience, statistical data, and so on) • Understands that personal experience, belief, and bias can influence critical thinking	• Distinguishes fact from interpretation when summarizing data • Explicates meaning (interprets) and evaluates significance (critical analysis) • Identifies crucial assumptions in reasoning • Uses evidence, applies logic, and constructs an argument for a proposed explanation and conclusion • Clearly articulates meaning or significance based on evidence • Uses interpolation, extrapolation, specific types of analysis, and inference • Identifies the difference between assumption and inference • Identifies potential influence of personal experience, belief, and bias on critical process	• Articulates what the data show through supporting statements of interpretation • Constructs an evidence-based explanation based on a connection between knowledge gained through investigation and an existing body of knowledge • Draws inferences characterized by deep understanding of content • Develops an independent interpretation based on evidence and appropriate methodology • Applies various critical approaches (postmodern, Marxist, and so on) appropriate to the task, advanced forms of discourse, and logical reasoning • Uses approaches drawn from areas of logic (inductive, abductive, and deductive reasoning)

continued →

Critical Thinking

Performance Area	Elementary	Middle	High
Draws conclusions, articulates patterns, and makes generalizations	• Avoids application of strict absolutism or overly loose relativism in drawing simplistic conclusions • Understands the differences among a generalization, principle, and law • Connects own reasoning process with the end result • Questions own reasoning and looks for gaps	• Determines which of several possible conclusions is most strongly supported by evidence and which should be rejected • Draws conclusions that reflect clear and logical links between the information or observations and the interpretations made from them • Identifies and reviews own reasoning in reaching a conclusion • Extends or generalizes conclusion to show broader application • Is able to communicate, document, and justify a position effectively	• Draws conclusions that are well reasoned, fully supported, and based on best analysis • Can determine which of several possible conclusions is most strongly warranted or supported by the evidence at hand and which should be rejected or regarded as less plausible • States the results of reasoning and justifies reasoning in terms of evidence and analysis • Argues convincingly using complex, coherent discussion of own perspective • Understands the difference between implication and consequence

Problem Solving

Performance Area	Elementary	Middle	High
Spots problems and is able to identify existing or potential problems	• Identifies problem and why it needs to be solved • Formulates questions or identifies problems relevant to the topic for the purpose of initiating inquiry and solving the problem (continued)	• Identifies problem, including a mention of the scope and need • Formulates questions to initiate and sustain an idea or investigation that has value in contexts outside the classroom (continued)	• States problem, convincingly defining the character and scope and establishing why it needs to be solved • Represents a problem in more than one way (continued)

	• Follows a scenario through various stages to identify potential problems • Identifies the underlying causes of problems	• Explores complex situations to uncover and articulate potential future problems • Identifies the underlying dynamics of a situation and applies systems thinking to understand the forces at work
	• Formulates questions that are clearly grounded in the issue, subject, or area of focus • Formulates questions that guide the investigation and reveal critical-thinking skills and prior knowledge • Explains why certain research techniques are important in drawing conclusions • Identifies gaps in understandings and searches broadly and thoroughly beyond the confines of the topic (parallel case studies, precedents, opposite scenarios, and so on) • Understands the nature and application of disciplinary thinking	• Formulates questions that generate complex discussion or hypotheses specific to a discipline or that span disciplines • Formulates questions that raise more questions about or provide insight into a topic, issue, problem, or idea, often revealing advanced critical-thinking skills and rich prior knowledge • Applies disciplinary knowledge and skills to direct and sustain the inquiry process • Demonstrates adaptability by changing the focus, questions, strategies, and position when necessary to achieve success
	• Identifies the contributing factors of a problem • Explores new topics to find solutions to understandable problems	
Devises a line of inquiry and follows an inquiry process	• Formulates and refines a range of questions to frame the search for new understanding relevant to the topic or discipline and uses structures or criteria for guidance • Designs and conducts an investigation based on defined strategy • Does not always accept the first answer, preferring to continue to probe and question • Asks new questions for continuing inquiry • Identifies the known and unknown elements of an issue • Identifies information needed to add to understanding of an issue or topic	

continued →

Problem Solving

Performance Area	Elementary	Middle	High
Manages information effectively and ethically	• Locates information from teacher-provided sources and from own observations and investigations • Makes basic determinations of source reliability • Chooses from several ways to connect and organize information and can use the most appropriate one for the circumstances • Identifies evidence and judges its merits and strengths for providing an explanation • Applies ethical judgment to the use and citation of resources and information	• Monitors gathered information and assesses for gaps or weaknesses • Synthesizes information and evidence gathered to answer questions • Uses organizational strategies to make sense of information • Distinguishes fact from interpretation when summarizing data or information • Infers meaning or significance of information based on evidence • Explains and justifies the process used to get information in appropriate formats • Locates information from diverse sources and points of view and demonstrates confidence and self-direction by making independent choices in the selection of resources and information • Evaluates information to determine its value and relevance for answering questions using set criteria • Acts on an understanding of the various types of ownership or licensing involved in knowledge products and resources	• Interprets information gathered from diverse sources by identifying misconceptions, conflicting information, point of view, and bias • Synthesizes knowledge gathered through inquiry with an existing body of knowledge • Manages information in more than one way, explains choices, and justifies decisions • Synthesizes and interprets rather than reports information • Demonstrates a highly ethical approach to the use and proper attribution of information, knowledge, ideas, and products • Demonstrates intellectual integrity

Develops a plan or prototype and tests it	• Creates simple models of ideas and solutions, graphical and physical • Discovers solutions beyond the obvious and explains the benefits of these solutions • Adapts and connects own ideas to suggestions to improve solutions for problems	• Creates prototype that is the most appropriate and achievable within the context of the problem and solution • Utilizes models to explain appropriateness of conclusion or solution • Develops plan to gather feedback by introducing prototype to audiences • Interprets feedback and refines design appropriately	• Designs prototypes that adequately illustrate the solution or conclusion • Mixes approaches to prototyping, including physical models, working models, conceptual models, case studies, simulations, and so on • Is able to use a range of strategies and tools to model a problem and understands that it may have more than one acceptable solution • Designs multiple prototypes for the solution or conclusion, focusing on multiple areas that will impact success (such as technical, economic, cultural, and so on)
Draws conclusions	• Connects solution or conclusion directly to the original problem • Articulates how the conclusion adequately addresses the problem or issue • Utilizes inferences, generalizations, and opinions appropriately • Articulates, documents, and justifies a position	• Develops well-founded conclusion based on objective consideration of prior ties across viable alternatives • Considers alternative methods, solutions, or perspectives and then selects and adequately tries out alternatives • Considers diverse and global perspectives in drawing conclusions • Draws conclusions from a variety of data resources to analyze and interpret • Creates *knowledge products* that adequately represent the blending of several information sources and expresses ideas beyond those referenced	• Constructs knowledge and moves toward better conclusions or greater confidence in conclusions • Creates knowledge products with high levels of creativity and insight that uniquely blend and extend the sources referenced • Anticipates the intended and unintended implications and limitations of conclusion • Identifies potential ethical issues inherent in the solution

continued →

Problem Solving

Performance Area	Elementary	Middle	High
Communicates solution and findings	• Communicates the processes used to reach solution and the related findings gathered through the inquiry • Presents, explains, and defends conclusions to an audience and explores possible consequences and further actions • Uses writing, speaking, and visual skills to communicate new knowledge or understandings effectively	• Communicates results in an appropriate manner for the audience and explains and justifies findings • Provides a clear summary of reasoning and process that leads to the solution selected • Provides some ideas about how own thinking has enhanced results • Justifies the conclusions reached in a fair-minded way, noting strengths and shortcomings • Engages audience in following a logical pathway to solution	• Communicates results, positions, and solutions in the most appropriate manner for audience and explains and justifies choice • Engages audience so that they care about the problem or issue the solution addresses • Clearly states the solution and convincingly proves that it is effective, feasible, and acceptable to those involved and better than alternatives • Anticipates and allows for likely objections, results, and consequences of the solution • Articulates solution limitations and how problem-solving approach and criteria can be refined, leading to better solutions or greater confidence over time • Explains in detail the sequence of thoughts used when facing a task or problem

Self-Directed Learning

Performance Area	Elementary	Middle	High
Analyzes past and ongoing performance	• Articulates understanding of acquired learning strategies • Demonstrates an awareness of own cognitive processes • Sets goals, monitors progress, and adjusts as needed • Describes challenges with tasks • Identifies successes and areas for attention in learning processes • Visualizes own thinking • Distinguishes between relevant and less-relevant information • Reviews information when meaning is not clear • Understands own learning style and effective modes of learning (such as auditory, visual, and so on) • Restates what is needed to complete a task and compares this with what is known • Applies simple strategies (skimming, rehearsing, and so on) to assist in learning effectiveness • Anticipates short-term steps involved in completing tasks	• Regulates cognitive processes through goal setting, monitoring, and controlling • Monitors comprehension of information and implements corrective strategies to improve comprehension • Reflects on achievement of goals • Identifies challenges in cognitive and interpersonal contexts • Self-assesses success of a task accurately • Uses strengths to compensate for weaknesses • Changes strategies when one does not work • Utilizes own learning style and effective modes of learning (such as auditory, visual, and so on) • Demonstrates high levels of self-regulation • Consciously attends to executive function skills as they pertain to the task • Recognizes when he or she lacks expertise and seeks to fill gaps • Anticipates medium-term steps involved in completing tasks	• Develops strategies to improve areas of weakness • Self-monitors the effectiveness of strategies applied • Optimizes information storage and retrieval routines • Consciously uses executive skills, such as extrapolation • Utilizes learned strategies to assist in completing challenging tasks • Uses metamemory approaches • Anticipates long-term needs of complex tasks

continued →

Self-Directed Learning

Performance Area	Elementary	Middle	High
Seeks and uses feedback	• Discusses potential strategies with others • Engages in think-alouds to receive feedback on thinking processes • Seeks help with difficult tasks • Self-questions • Checks goal setting and planning with others	• Interacts with peers to learn their strategies • Identifies who can support him or her with a particular aspect of his or her learning • Adjusts thinking processes based on feedback	• Uses feedback to test own beliefs • Synthesizes feedback from multiple sources • Optimizes learning processes by selectively applying feedback • Adapts and applies strategies observed in others
Adjusts thinking processes to new contexts	• Identifies the needs and context of a new learning challenge • Develops a specific plan when approaching new learning tasks • Demonstrates metacognitive awareness in both individual and group contexts • Works backward from desired goals to identify approaches and strategies	• Selects between different strategies for the most appropriate to the task • Controls the factors that influence his or her performance in unique environments • Uses models and mental organizers specific to the context	• Uses strategies to think about and solve new problems • Identifies impact of new information on own thinking • Applies declarative, procedural, and conditional knowledge appropriate to the task • Transfers metacognitive strategies across domains and environments
Attends to underlying beliefs	• Demonstrates active engagement in learning • Demonstrates increased self-confidence as a learner through the application of strategies • Recognizes personal strengths and limits regarding memory and other cognitive tasks • Sustains focus on tasks, goals, and planned processes	• Articulates a sense of accomplishment and personal self-satisfaction in his or her work • Demonstrates self-direction in learning tasks • Identifies self as a learner able to be successful in the face of challenges • Demonstrates motivation to learn a metacognitive strategy as a means of success • Affirms own ongoing processes verbally	• Demonstrates a high level of self-efficacy as a learner • Sees challenges as opportunities to grow as a learner • Demonstrates intrinsic motivation • Is determined to improve abilities as a learner in the completion of all academic tasks

Examples of Assessment Principles

Districts, schools, and departments should collaboratively develop shared understandings and agreements around the principles of effective assessment in their context. This allows the organization to own these principles and make the journey from principle to practice with a solid and common foundation. Following is a sample set of principles—that assessments are purposeful, well designed, and learning focused—based on those from the International School of Beijing. These principles were developed via a collaborative process between curriculum personnel and teachers.

Purposeful

The highest purpose of assessment is for students to demonstrate deep understandings through the application and transfer of knowledge and skills.

- Is it possible for my students to succeed on an assessment without showing evidence of the articulated understandings? Is this appropriate for an individual assessment?

- Could the performance be accomplished without in-depth understanding?

- Could the specific performance be poor, but could the student still understand the key ideas?

- Does my assessment design present students with novel contexts and tasks within which they can transfer their learning?

- Throughout my unit, is there an opportunity to assess whether students simply know the content or skill or they can also apply it purposefully and with transfer?

- What kind of real-world task would require someone to apply these understandings?

Assessment data, both qualitative and quantitative, are purposefully used to inform classroom practice and assist individual students in reaching their potential.

- What types of qualitative evidence can I gather that will show me the level of student understanding, application, or transfer?

- Does my team have agreed-on criteria (with consistent application) for the interpretation of qualitative performance data?

- Have I decided on the appropriate application of quantitative or qualitative assessment design for a specific goal?

Grading should provide a clear and consistent representation of student learning aligned with established and common performance standards.

- Are scoring tools developed with appropriate and clear criteria to evaluate student products and performances?

- Can we point to strengths and weaknesses based on performance criteria that align with the stated goals of the unit or assessment?

- Do we have measures to encourage consistent application of assessment criteria across classrooms?

Assessment addresses both formative and summative aspects of student growth and achievement.

- Are assessment opportunities spread throughout my unit?

- Have I used early assessment data to evaluate needed adjustments in class instruction or differentiation?

- Do I follow up quick checks for understanding with opportunities to fill the gaps for individual students?

Well Designed

Strong assessments involve complex tasks and allow for differentiation in the ways in which students will demonstrate their learning.

- Is there a variety of appropriate assessment tasks used to provide evidence of learning?

- Is there a way to ensure that different learners can demonstrate their learning in different ways?

- Are the potential tasks complex and varied enough to engage different learning styles?

Effective evidence of understanding requires multiple sources of evidence—a photo album, not a single snapshot.

- Is a variety of appropriate assessment tasks used to provide evidence of learning?

- Is the spread of assessment types appropriately broad across this unit?

- Do these assessment types ask for different demonstrations or facets of understanding?

Assessment should reflect a tight alignment between the learning goals identified and the evidence we plan to collect.

- Are the assessment tasks aligned with all elements of stage 1 (desired results) of the Understanding by Design framework, with the possible exception of essential questions?

- Does the task align with the stated essential understandings of the unit?

- Will students need to use the knowledge and skills listed in stage 1 to be successful at this task?

The tasks are designed to allow for the demonstration of advanced Learning21 (the International School of Beijing's model for modern learning) skills and to provide feedback on Learning21 skills.

- Which, if any, Learning21 skill is an important part of students being successful at this task?

- What observable and identifiable indicators for that skill are appropriate to this task?

- Can I include some of these indicators as success criteria for this task?

- How can I best capture demonstrations of these indicators?

- How can I provide purposeful feedback regarding the level of the Learning21 skill demonstrated and provide assistance for growth?

Learning Focused

Assessors identify where and how to look for different types of learning and facets of understanding via authentic, integrated, and contextualized performance.

- Have students asked to exhibit their understanding through authentic performance tasks?

- Have I addressed appropriate facets of understanding in my assessment design?

- Have I explored elements of goal, role, audience, situation, product, and standard (GRASPS) to inform the design of performance tasks?

- What different types of learning am I assessing in this unit or assessment? Recall or automation? Constructed learning?

- Does this task have relevance for my students?

Assessors include participation of students in identifying criteria and evaluating products.

- Are students aware of the criteria for success early on?

- Is there a benefit in having students suggest some criteria?

- Is there an opportunity for peer assessment?

Assessment feedback is a crucial element in student goal setting, metacognitive awareness, and motivation to learn and grow.

- Are students encouraged to self-assess and reflect?

- Is there a way to include this assessment experience to help students track their ongoing progress?

- Is there a way to ensure that the level of engagement is high enough to seed success?

- Is there an opportunity for students to observe and comment on their own learning processes?

Source: Adapted from the International School of Beijing, 2011. Used with permission.

References and Resources

Bergmann, J., & Sams, A. (2012, April 15). How the flipped classroom is radically transforming learning. *The Daily Riff.* Accessed at www.thedailyriff.com /articles/how-the-flipped-classroom-is-radically-transforming-learning-536 .php on December 10, 2014.

Brandt, R. (1998). *Powerful learning.* Alexandria, VA: Association for Supervision and Curriculum Development.

Bransford, J. D., Brown, A. L., & Cocking, R. R. (Eds.). (2000). *How people learn: Brain, mind, experience, and school* (Expanded ed.). Washington, DC: National Academies Press.

Costa, A. L., & Kallick, B. (Eds.). (2000). *Assessing and reporting on habits of mind.* Alexandria, VA: Association for Supervision and Curriculum Development.

Costa, A. L., & Kallick, B. (Eds.). (2008). *Learning and leading with habits of mind: 16 essential characteristics for success.* Alexandria, VA: Association for Supervision and Curriculum Development.

Crawford, M., Galiatsos, S., & Lewis, A. C. (2011). *The 1.0 guidebook to LDC: Linking secondary core content to the Common Core State Standards.* New York: Literacy Design Collaborative.

Curtis, G. (2015). *What is a vision without impacts?* [Web log post]. Accessed at http://gregcurtis-consulting.ca/dir/blog/2015/06/04/what-is-learning -without-impacts on June 9, 2015.

Darling-Hammond, L. (2014). Testing to, and beyond, the Common Core. *Principal, January/February*, 8–12. Accessed at www.naesp.org/sites/default /files/Darling-Hammond_JF14.pdf on January 19, 2015.

Darling-Hammond, L., & Falk, B. (2013). *Teacher learning through assessment: How student-performance assessments can support teacher learning.* Washington, DC: Center for American Progress. Accessed at http://cdn .americanprogress.org/wp-content/uploads/2013/09/TeacherLearning .pdf on December 10, 2014.

DuFour, R., DuFour, R., & Eaker, R. (2008). *Revisiting professional learning communities at work: New insights for improving schools.* Bloomington, IN: Solution Tree Press.

e-Learning Industry. (2014). *What is the future of education? Infographic.* Accessed at http://elearninginfographics.com/what-is-the-future-of-education-inf ographic/ on May 6, 2015.

Goldberg, G., & Roswell, B. (1998, April). *Perception and practice: The impact of teachers' scoring experience on performance-based instruction and classroom assessment.* Paper presented at the Annual Meeting of the American Educational Research Association, San Diego, CA.

Hattie, J. (2009). *Visible learning: A synthesis of over 800 meta-analyses relating to achievement.* New York: Routledge.

Jacobs, H. H. (1997). *Mapping the big picture: Integrating curriculum and assessment K–12.* Alexandria, VA: Association for Supervision and Curriculum Development.

Jacobs, H. H. (Ed.). (2004). *Getting results with curriculum mapping.* Alexandria, VA: Association for Supervision and Curriculum Development.

Jacobs, H. H. (Ed.). (2010). *Curriculum 21: Essential education for a changing world.* Alexandria, VA: Association for Supervision and Curriculum Development.

Jacobs, H. H. (Ed.). (2014a). *Leading the new literacies.* Bloomington, IN: Solution Tree Press.

Jacobs, H. H. (Ed.). (2014b). *Mastering digital literacy.* Bloomington, IN: Solution Tree Press.

Jacobs, H. H. (Ed.). (2014c). *Mastering global literacy.* Bloomington, IN: Solution Tree Press.

Jacobs, H. H. (Ed.). (2014d). *Mastering media literacy.* Bloomington, IN: Solution Tree Press.

KnowledgeWorks. (2012). *KnowledgeWorks forecast 3.0: Recombinant education—Regenerating the learning ecosystem.* Accessed at http://knowledgeworks.org /download/file/fid/793 on December 18, 2014.

KnowledgeWorks Foundation. (2006). *2006–2016 map of future forces affecting education.* Accessed at http://resources.knowledgeworks.org/map on December 10, 2014.

KnowledgeWorks Foundation. (2008). *2020 forecast: Creating the future of learning.* Accessed at www.knowledgeworks.org/sites/default/files/2020-Forecast.pdf on December 10, 2014.

Literacy Design Collaborative. (2014). *LDC task template collection version 3.0.* Accessed at http://ldc.org/sites/default/files/ldc-resource-library-files /LDC%20Task%20Template%20Collection%20v3.%2012-1-14.pdf on June 9, 2015.

Marzano, R. J., Pickering, D. J., & McTighe, J. (1993). *Assessing student outcomes: Performance assessment using the dimensions of learning model.* Alexandria, VA: Association for Supervision and Curriculum Development.

Marzano, R. J., Pickering, D. J., & Pollock, J. E. (2001). *Classroom instruction that works: Research-based strategies for increasing student achievement.* Alexandria, VA: Association for Supervision and Curriculum Development.

McTighe, J. (2008). Making the most of professional learning communities. *The Learning Principal, 3*(8), 1, 4–7.

McTighe, J. (2013). *Core learning: Assessing what matters most.* Midvale, UT: School Improvement Network.

McTighe, J., & Lyman, F. T., Jr. (1988). Cueing thinking in the classroom: The promise of theory-embedded tools. *Educational Leadership, 45*(7), 18–24.

McTighe, J., & March, T. (2015). Choosing apps by design. *Educational Leadership, 72*(8), 36–41.

McTighe, J., & Seif, E. (2010). An implementation framework to support 21st century skills. In J. A. Bellanca & R. Brandt (Eds.), *21st century skills: Rethinking how students learn* (pp. 149–172). Bloomington, IN: Solution Tree Press.

McTighe, J., & Wiggins, G. (2013). *Essential questions: Opening doors to student understanding.* Alexandria, VA: Association for Supervision and Curriculum Development.

Miller, A. (2012, February 24). *Five best practices for the flipped classroom* [Web log post]. Accessed at www.edutopia.org/blog/flipped-classroom-best-practices-andrew-miller on December 10, 2014.

Milton, J. (2005). *Who was Ronald Reagan?* New York: Grosset & Dunlap.

Montgomery County Public Schools. (2013). *Learning for the future: A parent's guide to kindergarten curriculum 2.0.* Accessed at http://205.222.0.20/upload dFiles/curriculum/elementary/parent-guide-traditional-kindergarten-en.pdf on December 4, 2014.

National Governors Association Center for Best Practices & Council of Chief State School Officers. (2010a). *Common Core State Standards for English language arts and literacy in history/social studies, science, and technical subjects.* Washington, DC: Authors. Accessed at www.corestandards.org/assets /CCSSI_ELA%20Standards.pdf on December 10, 2014.

National Governors Association Center for Best Practices & Council of Chief State School Officers. (2010b). *Common Core State Standards for mathematics.* Washington, DC: Authors. Accessed at www.corestandards.org/assets /CCSSI_Math%20Standards.pdf on December 10, 2014.

National Research Council. (2012). *Education for life and work: Developing transferable knowledge and skills in the 21st century.* Washington, DC: National Academies Press.

Newmann, F., Bryk, A., & Nagaoka, J. (2001). *Authentic intellectual work and standardized tests: Conflict or coexistence?* Chicago: Consortium on Chicago School Research.

NGSS Lead States. (2013). *Next Generation Science Standards: For states, by states.* Washington, DC: National Academies Press. Accessed at www .dseducationfoundation.org/documents/2013/08/nexgen-dev-2.pdf on January 19, 2015.

Partnership for 21st Century Skills. (2007). *Assessment of 21st century skills.* Accessed at www.p21.org/storage/documents/Assessment092806.pdf on December 10, 2014.

Partnership for 21st Century Skills. (2009). *P21 framework definitions.* Washington, DC: Author. Accessed at www.p21.org/storage/documents/P21_Framework _Definitions.pdf on December 10, 2014.

Tokuhama-Espinosa, T. (2010). *The new science of teaching and learning: Using the best of mind, brain, and education science in the classroom.* New York: Teachers College Press.

Tomlinson, C. A., & McTighe, J. (2006). *Integrating differentiated instruction and understanding by design: Connecting content and kids.* Alexandria, VA: Association for Supervision and Curriculum Development.

Tyler, R. W. (1949). *Basic principles of curriculum and instruction.* Chicago: University of Chicago Press.

University of Pennsylvania. (n.d.). *The GRIT survey* [Web survey]. Accessed at https:// sasupenn.qualtrics.com/SE/?SID=SV_06f6QSOS2pZW9qR on December 10, 2014.

Wack, P. (1985). Scenarios: Uncharted waters ahead. *Harvard Business Review.* Accessed at https://hbr.org/1985/09/scenarios-uncharted-waters-ahead on June 9, 2015.

Wiggins, G., & McTighe, J. (2005). *Understanding by design* (Expanded 2nd ed.). Alexandria, VA: Association for Supervision and Curriculum Development.

Wiggins, G., & McTighe, J. (2007). *Schooling by design: Mission, action, and achievement.* Alexandria, VA: Association for Supervision and Curriculum Development.

Wiggins, G., & McTighe, J. (2011). *The understanding by design guide to creating high-quality units.* Alexandria, VA: Association for Supervision and Curriculum Development.

Wiggins, G., & McTighe, J. (2012). *The understanding by design guide to advanced concepts in creating and reviewing units.* Alexandria, VA: Association for Supervision and Curriculum Development.

Wiliam, D. (2007/2008). Changing classroom practice. *Educational Leadership*, *65*(4), 36–42.

Willis, J. (2006). *Research-based strategies to ignite student learning: Insights from a neurologist and classroom teacher*. Alexandria, VA: Association for Supervision and Curriculum Development.

Zmuda, A., Curtis, G., & Ullman, D. (2015). *Learning personalized: The evolution of the contemporary classroom*. San Francisco: Jossey-Bass.

Index

Stop Leading Like It's Yesterday!
By Casey Reason
Explore the Leading for Excellence and Fulfillment model, and discover practical, research-based strategies that will be relevant to school leaders today and tomorrow. Integrate ready-to-use leadership techniques that will open up an unprecedented world of opportunities for both students and teachers.
BKF614

Deeper Learning
Edited by James A. Bellanca
Education authorities from around the globe draw on research as well as their own experience to explore deeper learning, a process that promotes higher-order thinking, reasoning, and problem solving to better educate students and prepare them for college and careers.
BKF622

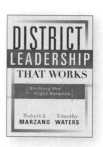

District Leadership That Works
By Robert J. Marzano and Timothy Waters
Bridge the divide between administrative duties and daily classroom impact with a leadership mechanism called *defined autonomy*. Learn strategies for creating district-defined goals while giving building-level staff the stylistic freedom to respond quickly and effectively to student failure.
BKF314

Game Plan
By Héctor García, Katherine McCluskey, and Shelley Taylor
Foreword by Richard DuFour
Create a uniform game plan to foster a collaborative community of learners, develop a shared focus, and meet growth goals. Explore coaching points you can use to customize strategies for teachers and leaders, who must share collective responsibility to drive lasting change.
BKF635

Solution Tree | Press *a division of* Solution Tree

Visit solution-tree.com or call 800.733.6786 to order.

Wait! Your professional development journey doesn't have to end with the last pages of this book.

We realize improving student learning doesn't happen overnight. And your school or district shouldn't be left to puzzle out all the details of this process alone.

No matter where you are on the journey, we're committed to helping you get to the next stage.

Take advantage of everything from **custom workshops** to **keynote presentations** and **interactive web and video conferencing**. We can even help you develop an action plan tailored to fit your specific needs.

Let's get the conversation started.

Call 888.763.9045 today.

solution-tree.com